SLEEK & SAVAGE

SLEEK & SAVAGE

NORTH AMERICA'S WEASEL FAMILY

by

DELPHINE HALEY

715 Harrison Street, Seattle, WA 98109

Cover and Page Design by Lou Rivera

Drawings by Maxine Morse

Cover: An ermine in winter coat
      Photo by Ed Cesar

⟨

First printing, December 1975
Copyright © 1975 by Pacific Search
International Standard Book Number 0-914718-12-6
Library of Congress Catalog Card Number 75-32837
Printed in the U.S.A.

Acknowledgments

This book was written with the help of many people. In particular, I wish to thank Dr. Neil F. Payne, University of Wisconsin College of Natural Resources at Stevens Point, and Dale Rice, National Marine Fisheries Service in Seattle for review of the manuscript, and Mack Hopkins for his editorial assistance. Others kindly furnished information, references, criticism, time and good will: Steve Bayless, Montana State Game Department, Helena; Dave Books, University of Montana School of Forestry, Missoula; Charles Bruce, Oregon Wildlife Commission, Portland; John Burns, Alaska Department of Fish and Game, Fairbanks; Dr. Victor H. Cahalane, formerly National Parks Chief Biologist and Associate Director of the New York State Museum, Albany; trapper Frank Conibear, inventor of the "instant kill" humane trap, Victoria, B.C.; Michael Dederer, The Seattle Fur Exchange; Dr. Ray Erickson, Assistant Director for Endangered Wildlife Research, U.S. Fish and Wildlife Service, Laurel, Maryland; Howard Hash, University of Idaho Cooperative Wildlife Research Unit, Moscow; Conrad H. Hillman, U.S. Fish and Wildlife Service, Rapid City, South Dakota; Dr. Lloyd G. Ingles, Fresno, California; Bill Irvine, Huron-Manistee National Forest, Cadillac, Michigan; Ron Jamison, U. S. Fish and Wildlife Service, Corvallis, Oregon; Murray Johnson, M.D., Tacoma, Washington; Karl Kenyon, U.S. Fish and Wildlife Service, Seattle; Jack Mandel, Hudson's Bay Company, New York City; Dr. Bruce Mate, Marine Science Center, Newport, Oregon; Glenn Maxham, Maxham Film Productions, Duluth, Minnesota; Roger Powell, University of Chicago Biology Department; Dick Randall, Defenders of Wildlife, Rock Springs, Wyoming; R. A. Rausch, Alaska Department of Fish and Game, Anchorage; B. J. Rose, South Dakota Department of Game, Fish and Parks, Pierre; Jim Tabor, Oregon State University Department of Fish and Wildlife, Corvallis; Thomas Thodus, Vancouver Raw Fur Auction, B.C.; G. W. West, B. C. Department of Wildlife, Burnaby; Dr. Charles F. Yocom, California State University College of Forestry and Wildlife, Arcata.

COLOR PLATES — PHOTOS BY:

BLACK AND WHITE PHOTOS BY:

*By permission of Stanford University Press, Figures 220 and 228 from *Mammals of the Pacific States* by Lloyd G. Ingles, 1965.

Preface

Many people disdain the small and secretive mustelids — mink, marten, weasel, ferret, skunk, and others — except for those bearing glamorous, expensive pelts. Some members of the weasel family have acquired unlovely reputations; the weasel and ferret are notorious as savage, often wanton killers, and the wolverine is reputed to have only one motivation — a hatred for mankind and his possessions. In addition, the mustelids are inextricably linked with a foul odor; beyond question, this is true whether the scent is sprayed or merely released into the air.

Author-naturalist Delphine Haley looks behind this public reputation, perceiving the many admirable features of the Family Mustelidae. One of the oldest living families of carnivores, it is highly successful. Even now, 35 million years after branching off from the ancestral stock of fissipeds, mustelids are still numerous. (The few rarities, such as the black-footed ferret, may well have been scarce even in prehistoric times.)

As another mark of success in mustelid evolution, scientists recognize twenty-five living genera and nearly seventy species found throughout the entire northern world, Africa, and South America. They live in varied habitats from the frozen tundra of extreme northern Greenland (home of the ermine) to the steamy jungles of South America (tayra and grison) and Sumatra (the stink badger). Although most mustelids are terrestrial, others are skilled climbers, spending much of their time in trees; some (the river otter and mink) are semiaquatic, and one — the sea otter — remains at sea for days at a time. By and large, mustelids are carnivorous. However, the diet of some includes plant material and fruit such as bananas (the tayra). Because of a fondness for honey, the ratel of Africa and Asia has been named the honey badger.

To some people, these mustelids are chicken-killers; to others, they are a livelihood. To all of us, they are valuable as a check on rodent populations. The following pages will open a window on an unusual group of mammals, the North American mustelids.

Victor H. Cahalane,
author of *Mammals of North America,* is a former National Parks Chief Biologist and Associate Director of the New York State Museum, Albany.

Table of Contents

Introduction

North America is the habitat for some magnificent carnivores. Grizzly bears roam the meadows and remote forests of Alaska, British Columbia, and Yukon Territory, while a few hundred more still survive farther south in the national parks of Glacier and Yellowstone. The mighty Kodiak, king of them all, fishes the streams of southeast Alaska. Cougars stalk the canyons and high country of Idaho, and black bears go a-berrying along Washington's Olympic Peninsula. In spite of man, the wolf still survives in Alaska and across northern Canada, with some still persisting in the western and northern Lake States.

Less spectacular but more numerous than their dramatic relatives are the smaller carnivores that quietly but determinedly maintain a vital place within the ecosystem. Among these are a highly specialized and ferocious family — the Mustelidae. They are formidable killers, known for their voracious appetites and vicious dispositions. Secretive and spry, relatively little known, they are the most widely distributed mammalian predators on the continent. As such, they provide the valuable service of controlling a variety of populations, including insects, rodents, and rabbits.

North American mustelids include three types of sleekly shaped weasel; mink, marten, and fisher; the ungainly badger and wolverine; four distressingly familiar kinds of skunk; those delightful clowns of the kingdom, the river and sea otters; and probably the rarest mammal on the continent, the black-footed ferret.

The family Mustelidae appears to have evolved in the early Oligocene epoch, thirty-six million years ago, in North America and Eurasia from a stock also ancestral to the Canidae, Ursidae, and Procyonidae (dog, bear, and raccoon). They are considered more primitive in many respects than the other families, tending to be comparatively small with short, stocky limbs. What they lack in size, however, is offset by a common strain of ferocity and aggressiveness unequaled in any other family.

Since the business of being a killer is a highly competitive as well as highly skilled occupation, these animals, like other carnivores, are designed to be efficient predators. R. F. Ewer has pointed out in her book, *The Carnivores,* that although the felids are usually regarded as the killers *par excellence,* on a lesser scale, the weasel killing a rabbit is no less worthy of respect than a lion bringing down a wildebeest. Equipped with powerful canine teeth and well-developed cutting carnassials, the musteline jaws are short and strong for a fast and fatal bite. For grinding up food, family members have one molar on each side of the upper jaw and two molars on each side of the lower jaw, while the number of premolars varies with the needs of each species. Within each genus, there is adaptive variety. Among the skunks, for instance, the more predacious spotted skunk has longer carnassials than the hognosed skunk, whose poorly developed carnassials are aided by a long snout for rooting after beetles and grubs.

Weasel family members share other general characteristics. Their body design is long and low, streamlined for quick movement and chasing prey down burrows. They all have short legs with five toes on each foot; they walk either on their toes (digitigrade) or somewhat on the flat of the foot (semiplantigrade). All except the sea otter have potent musk glands that are used to attract a mate or repel an enemy, a feature that reaches its highest development in the skunk, the only species to spray its scent for any distance. (However, it is claimed that the skunk's odor is far less offensive than that of an angry mink.) Smell is their most highly developed sense, followed by hearing and sight.

12

In many of these animals, the development of the fetus is delayed until the most favorable time for birth. Apparently, all but two weasel family members, the striped skunk and the least weasel, undergo this process known as delayed implantation, although this has not yet been specifically determined for the black-footed ferret or the hooded and hognosed skunks. The marten, for instance, has a gestation period of about 259 days. After mating in July or August, the fertilized egg develops for a few days and then lies unimplanted in the uterus until January. At that time, the blastocyst is implanted and, after about 50 days of development, birth occurs in March. Of the 259 days' gestation, only about 52 are spent in actual development of the offspring.

Delayed implantation, which also occurs in some species of bears, seems to be influenced by photoperiod, i.e., light duration. In lower latitudes, the gestation period for a given species is shorter, although the period of internal development remains the same. Studies at the U.S. Fur Farm Experimental Station in Saratoga, New York, have shown that increased daylight in spring stimulates embryonic development. Further experiments under artificial circumstances reveal that by increasing the amount of light in the fall, delay of implantation of the blastocyst can be shortened by as much as three months.

Gestation for the mustelids may vary from 39 days for the mink to 352 days for the fisher. Though they usually have only one litter a year, the number of offspring in a litter can range from one for the sea otter to thirteen for the short-tailed weasel.

Mustelids are difficult to observe and study because of their erratic natures, varied habitats, and nocturnal habits. Much of the information about them comes from trappers, who are experienced in recognizing their different tracks and observing their signs during snowy seasons.

As with any successful group venture, diversification is important. Different diets and habitats ensure survival. While the more arboreal mustelids — the martens and fishers — eat squirrels, nuts, and fruits, the two marine mustelids — the sea otter and the river otter — dine on fish and mollusks. The wolverine climbs the high mountains, eating anything it can find, while the badger digs for gophers or other den dwellers in the dry desert areas. The ubiquitous plume-tailed skunks are virtually untroubled by predators as they wander throughout the lower elevations feeding on a varied diet of insects or fruit. Most carnivorous are the weasels which, along with the mink, are a plague to the farmer. However, this destructive activity is easily offset by the weasel's important role as rodent controller. In areas where these small carnivores have been eliminated, plagues from rodents or diseases from rabbits have often resulted.

Collectively, the members of the weasel family wear the finest and most lustrous fur coats in North America. Indeed, most of this continent was explored and initially developed because of the persistent demand for these furs. The winter coat of the short-tailed weasel in "ermine" phase and the lustrous pelts of fishers, marten, and mink have long been symbols of luxury throughout the world. Wolverine fur is used as trim for parkas in the Far North; even the striped skunk has achieved some popularity with the decline of its less musky brothers. Topping the list is the sea otter, whose richly colored, dense — and expensive — fur is unrivaled as the finest in the world.

Considering the severe pressures of man's lust for fur — a wave of trapping and tanning that spread across the continent, lasting well into the twentieth century when the harvests finally dropped off — it is remarkable that some of these species survived at all. In recent years, rodent poisons have taken their toll of the mustelids, and survival space is shrinking as a result of man's civilizing activities. The black-footed ferret is all but gone, though it may never have existed in great numbers. The wolverine, that solitary denizen of the wilderness, has become even scarcer than it was originally. The marten and fisher have managed to survive only in greatly reduced numbers and habitat. Weasels, skunks, badgers, and mink appear to be plentiful enough, as is the river otter. After the threat of almost certain extinction, the sea otter has reestablished itself along our coastline.

In typical fashion, the mustelids have even insinuated themselves into our vocabulary, suggesting all of the furtive, smart, and aggressive characteristics of the tribe: to ferret out information, to badger into submission, or to weasel out of a situation — even to defeat an opponent thoroughly by skunking him — all are part of the mustelid mystique.

The weasel family is persistent — a hardy breed. Poisons, traps, hunters and loggers, fluctuations of prey, and loss of habitat have all had an impact on these animals. With the same tenacity that they display as individuals, the group may be lucky enough to keep a firm grip on their important niche in the ecosystem.

Long-Tailed Weasel *(Mustela frenata)*
Short-Tailed Weasel *(Mustela erminea)*
Least Weasel *(Mustela nivalis)*

Mustela erminea

"If this creature were as large as a cougar, nobody would dare to venture out of doors, because it is second to none, including the badger, in courage, and is possibly the most bloodthirsty villain on earth." Thus an Idaho biologist describes the weasel. Tooth for tooth and ounce for ounce, the weasel is the fiercest and most efficient predator in the mammal world.

Three weasel species are found in North America. Largest is the long-tailed weasel, *Mustela frenata*, which reaches up to twenty-four inches in length (depending upon subspecies and sex) and weighs six to nine ounces. Next in size, and often mistaken for its long-tailed relative, is the short-tailed weasel, *Mustela erminea*, which measures eight to thirteen inches and weighs considerably less — only two to four ounces. Difficult as it may be to imagine

15

a smaller species, there is one: *Mustela nivalis,* the least weasel, which is seven to eight inches long and weighs in at one or two ounces. It is the smallest carnivore in the world.

These small carnivores compensate for their diminutive size through a combination of agility, strength, and sheer nerve. A three-inch-high weasel, if blocked or driven from a kill, will attack anything — even man. Its deadly aggression is legendary.

Zoologist Osmond Breland, in his book *Animal Life and Lore,* claims that weasels appear to kill for the sheer joy of it. They have been known to destroy entire colonies of rats and are sometimes forced to change residence because they have eliminated all of the natural prey in the area. As an example, Breland lists the contents found in one small weasel's nest: eight dead mice plus the remains of six other rodents. He also tells of a biologist who, while tracking a weasel through the snow, found the remains of eleven rabbits along its trail. In another instance, the skull of one tenacious (and ambitious) weasel was found with its teeth imbedded in the neck of an eagle.

When its sensitive nose and keen eyes pick up prey, the weasel's head sways a little and its eyes glitter with greed. Quickly it pounces on the victim, pins it to the ground, and bites into the neck or the base of the brain case. Mammalogist Walter Dalquest described such an incident when he came upon a weasel pursuing a young snowshoe rabbit along the edge of a highway near Forks, Washington: "The weasel dashed from cover to intercept the rabbit in the center of the road. It knocked the rabbit to its side and, placing its feet on the rabbit's shoulders, bit fiercely at its neck . . . . [The rabbit] then stood up, made two hops and died."

Overly fierce as weasels may appear, there is reason for this behavior: they require up to 40 percent of their body weight in food every day. Most of this is meat, for they are the most carnivorous of all the mustelids. Contrary to popular belief, they are not bloodsuckers. They will kill more than they can eat but will usually store their surplus for future use. By design, weasels are shaped for entering narrow spaces for prey. Research conducted by University of California scientists in 1972 on the long-tailed weasel shows that these animals pay a high price for being long and thin. Experiments revealed that the metabolism of "cold stressed" weasels is 50 to 100 percent greater than that of other normally shaped animals of the same weight. Weasels have greater surface area and shorter fur, and are not able to gain

When its sensitive nose and keen eyes pick up prey, the long-tailed weasel's eyes glitter with greed.

spherical resting posture. Thus, in evolving an elongate shape, they have sacrificed some efficiency in using their energy.

Small rodents are their staple diet, garnished with rabbits, birds, eggs, reptiles, amphibians, insects, and worms. The diet of the least weasel is limited almost entirely to mice. Its larger relatives have been known to raid henhouses and slaughter whole flocks, much to the fury of the farmer. Nevertheless, these animals are a boon to him. As a principal predator of harmful rodents, they are more effective than any mousetrap in protecting fields and orchards from meadow mice, rats, and pocket gophers. It has been claimed that, were it not for weasels, rats and mice would multiply so rapidly that they would overrun the earth. A population estimate for New York State lists approximately 300,000 weasels, which eliminate 60 million rats and mice each year. Appropriately, the generic name for weasels, *Mustela,* means "those who carry off mice."

In turn, these little carnivores are preyed upon by their own relatives — mink, marten, and fishers — as well as by bobcats, coyotes, wolves, owls, and hawks. When attacked, they resort to speed and the ability to enter tiny escape holes where attackers cannot follow.

Hyperactive, superaggressive, the weasel is so high-strung that some in captivity have died from overexcitement. Rather than walk, it darts, swift and snakelike, in and out of crevices. Rather than run, it makes a series of small bounds, arching its back and contracting its body until its four feet, for an instant, are close together. Sometimes when it scurries among the rockpiles or through the brush tirelessly searching for food, it stops and stands erect, peering about with a suspicious and curious look on its tiny face — a canny little creature in a camouflage of soft fur.

Summer or winter, the weasel is difficult to spot, not only because of its furtive movements, but also because of its beautifully blending coat. Through natural selection, the northern weasel has gained the capacity to exchange its summer brown coat for winter white. These molts, which occur generally in the more snow-covered northern ranges, are triggered by the changing duration of daylight. The amount of light received through the eyes is believed to influence the pituitary gland, which in turn affects the hormones controlling the molting cycle. Thus, in March or April, new dark hairs appear on the weasel's back and gradually extend down the flanks until the upper parts turn brown. In winter the process reverses to white.

Ermine, the fur of kings, is the weasel's natural winter coat. Its soft, white pelt, with black tails symbolizing the highest rank, adorns the capes of Europe's royalty. The British have used vast quantities of the black and white ermine pelts for coronation robes; as many as 50,000 of these little furs were shipped from Canada for the coronation of King George in 1937. Though today the pelts of the short-tailed weasel in ermine phase are less in demand,

The short-tailed weasel caught with its prey.

they are still used as trim for collars and cuffs. Prices vary with size and quality: in 1973-74 from 35¢ to $2.00 for the short-tailed pelts, from 60¢ to $3.25 for the long-tailed.

All three weasels produce a variety of small noises when frightened or angered. They bark, shriek, hiss, or snarl, but usually cannot be heard by man unless they are enraged. Man does take immediate notice, however, when an angry weasel unleashes a spray of foul-smelling musk. The musk is also used to mark off territory — an effective No Trespassing sign — or as a lure from a female to entice a mate.

Weasels establish home ranges varying in size from a couple of acres to many miles, depending on the food available. However, they do not normally travel over long distances. In 1933, a tracking study in fresh snow established the short-tailed weasel's range at 4 miles; another study in 1944 established it at 3.43 miles. Always there are exceptions: in 1960, a large male weasel was tagged and released 8 miles from the village of Nunapitchuk, Alaska. Eight months later, it was caught near another village raiding a fish trap. The airline distance between the points of release and capture was 22 miles. According to the Alaska Department of Fish and Game, people in this area often speak of large-scale movements of mink and weasels over this larger terrain. Another record was established in 1956 when a frozen and mummified carcass of *Mustela erminea* was found at the 15,000-foot level of Mt. McKinley, 2 vertical miles above timberline. It was concluded that the weasel had traveled there under its own power before dying, presumably of starvation.

Within its home range, the weasel fashions a den, often lining it with trophies of the hunt — bones, fur, feathers, or dried meat. Almost any sheltered place will do — a rockpile, stump, log, burrow, the understructure of a barn, or an old building.

The long-tailed weasel is the most common of the tribe. Its specific name, *frenata,* is derived from the Latin word for bridle (*frenum*), referring to the dark mask worn by those in the more southerly parts of its range. Squirrel-sized, it is about half as large as the mink or marten and twice the size of the short-tailed weasel. While the range of its smaller relatives extends across Europe and Asia, *M. frenata* is exclusively North American, where it is found along the shrubby borders of farmlands, in grassy plains and forests, wherever food and water are available. Only the higher latitudes of Alaska

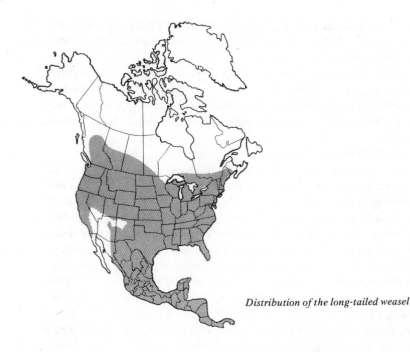

Distribution of the long-tailed weasel

and the Canadian provinces are unsuitable as habitat, as is a small portion of the arid southwest United States. The long-tailed weasel was also formerly absent from the southern tip of Florida, but there is a 1972 record of this species found in the cypress sloughs of subtropical Florida along the Tamiami Trail.

In summer, the long-tailed weasel's coat is brown above with a yellowish white or buff color stretching below from chin to groin. Its feet are brown. In the northerly parts of its range, such as the mountains of the Sierra Nevada or in colder areas east of the Cascades of Oregon, Washington, and British Columbia, its winter coat turns to white. In warmer coastal areas and at lower latitudes, the winter fur stays brown or remains only slightly paler than it does in summer. The tail is marked with a black tip in all seasons.

The long-tailed weasel mates in July or August, followed by a gestation period (due to delayed implantation) of about 279 days, or 9 months. A litter

of four to nine is born in April or May. At birth the little long-tails are tiny —
one-ninth of an ounce — but they develop quickly. For the weaker weasel,
mortality at this critical stage is high. By the end of the third week, their fur
has thickened and they have been introduced to solid food. Their eyes usually
open in five weeks, about the time weaning is completed. At two months, they
follow their mother like a pack of tiny hounds while she ferrets out food for
the family. Fast to mature, female weasels born in spring will mate the same
fall, but males may wait until the following year.

The short-tailed weasel, commonly called the ermine, closely resembles
M. frenata except for its smaller size. In addition, it has a tiny white line on
the inside of the hind leg which extends to its completely white feet. The ermine is found over a larger range, extending across the northern United
States and throughout Canada. Colored chocolate above in summer, its coat
turns white in winter throughout its range, except on the humid northwest

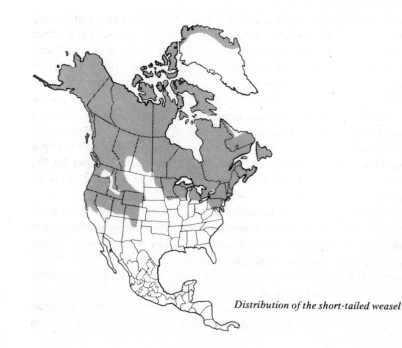

Distribution of the short-tailed weasel

coast from southern British Columbia to California, where it remains brown for the entire year. Throughout its range, the short-tailed weasel is most numerous at lower elevations where there is water and a plentiful food supply of small mammals and birds.

At birth in springtime, the four to seven young short-tails weigh only one-fourteenth of an ounce. Each is fed by both parents and develops at about the same rate as its long-tailed cousin. As it matures, this weasel leads a more active life than the night-loving long-tail, for it can be found hunting at any hour. It has a way of disappearing under one's very eyes, especially when camouflaged in its winter coat, but a network of crisscrossing trails gives evidence that it is on the prowl. The ermine, more agile and ambitious, also climbs and swims with greater frequency than does the long-tailed weasel. Both species are subject to marked population fluctuations that reach a peak every four to seven years and then drop off drastically. This phenomenon is most frequent in Canada and Alaska, where weasels are subject to the rise and fall of rodent populations.

The two-ounce least weasel is identified by its diminutive size and its very short tail (one to one and one-half inches long), which is without the distinct black tip. From the Alleghenies across the continent to Alaska, it is found most often in marshes, meadows, and open woodlands. Only in the southeast part of its range does it remain brown in winter. In northern British Columbia, this little weasel is found sparsely in parkland-type habitats. Here and in the brushy country of Alaska, where it occurs in larger numbers, it has a curious dependence on mice for more than its diet. At breeding time, which apparently can happen in any season, the least weasel mother will usurp a mouse nest. This she lines with mouse fur, preparing a cozy chamber for the three to ten wee weasels she will produce. The least weasel father takes no part in rearing the young.

The young mature quickly and begin the hectic hunting pace of all their kind. However, this little mammal probably packs more nervous energy into its tiny body than any other. In 1930, biologist Richard Nelson wrote: "Once when camping in spring among scattered snowbanks on the coast of the Bering Sea, I had an excellent opportunity to witness their almost incredible quickness. Early in the morning one suddenly appeared on the margin of a snowbank within a few feet. After craning its neck one way and the other as though to get a better view of me, it vanished, only to reappear so abruptly on a snowbank three or four yards away that it was almost impossible to follow it with the eye . . . certainly no other mammal can have such flashlike powers of movement."

Along with its small size goes a tiny territory, usually no more than two acres. The least weasel can cover this range by skittering along the surface or burrowing beneath the snow, always in quick pursuit of meadow mice. In times of extreme hunger, it has been known to attack squirrels, rats, and even young cottontails, fearlessly ignoring their larger size.

In Eskimo tradition, a father sometimes fastens the head and skin of a least weasel to his small son's belt so that the young hunter will absorb some of the "little chief's" fiery spirit. Considering the least weasel's deadly aggression, this might be more than any young Eskimo boy would want to bargain for.

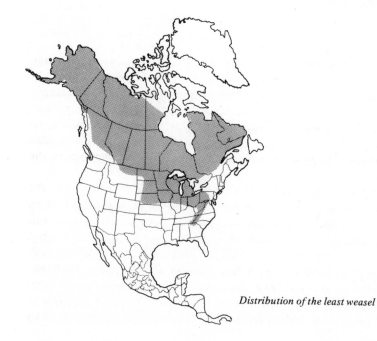

Distribution of the least weasel

Mink *(Mustela vison)*

The mink (*Mustela vison*) is almost as predacious as the weasel. Though this sleek, dark animal is not quite as fast as its relative, it is still speedy by any standards — a versatile hunter on land or in stream. The mink in turn is preyed upon by man, for it wears one of the most beautiful coats of any mammal. In fact, the mink was the first American furbearer to be raised commercially when fur farming began just before the Civil War. Today this animal is probably the best known and most glamorized member of the weasel family.

Apart from the dubious honor of becoming a fur coat in later life, the mink spends its daily existence secretly prowling alone like others of its family. Weighing from one and one-half to four pounds, it is a low-built animal, about as long as a housecat (nineteen to twenty-eight inches), but much more slender. One-third of its sleek length is taken up by a fluffy tail. Its head is small, with close-set ears barely visible above the fur. Its beady black eyes are bright as it hurries about in search of prey, stretching a long, sinuous neck to peek around corners and over rocks. Webbed feet enable it to swim well, for the mink is seldom far from water. Although sometimes it can

Semiaquatic, the mink can readily catch fast-swimming fish.

be spotted along the water's edge in daytime, it prefers to roam at night. At other times, only its tracks indicate that it has been fishing along a riverbank.

Mink are found near water across North America. The Northwest's dry Columbia plateau, the southwest desert, the far northern Arctic Slope and Barren Grounds are not suitable areas for this aquaphile. Within its remaining rich habitat of marshes, mountain streams, reedy banks, ocean beaches, and even city ponds, the mink lives on a diverse diet. Semiaquatic, it can readily catch fast-swimming fish in a stream or dive for crayfish on the bottom. It consumes a variety of both vertebrates and invertebrates along the marshy banks or at seaside — salamanders, frogs, or snakes, even dead fish washed up on the beach. The menu changes with its habitat, ranging from ducks on Seattle's Lake Washington to sticklebacks along the inlets of Alaska, wood ducks in Illinois, waterfowl in Michigan, or muskrat in North Carolina.

The mink is also a dry-land forager of some repute. Widely nomadic except when rearing young, it travels overland in search of meadow mice, rabbits, rats, or squirrels, tracking its prey by scent. Males will cover several square miles within a year and select temporary housing along the way in a borrowed burrow or a hole in a bank, while females usually move about much less. The mink is not even averse to a little tree climbing to search for birds' eggs. Aloft, it is sometimes fleet enough to catch a bird, a feathery feast which it often plucks before devouring.

In Alaska, mink are abundant along the coast, particularly along the Kuskokwim Delta and the beaches of Kotzebue Sound. Records of fifteen mink per linear mile of beach in southeast Alaska are not uncommon. Inland they can occur some distance from rivers and streams as long as there are high populations of mice and hares available. However, such is not always the case. According to Alaska biologist John Burns, the 1974 hare population fell

Distribution of the mink

27

off drastically, and trappers have reported that the mink were having to return to traditional water courses for a more stable diet of fishes and insects.

Muskrat is a favorite mink meal. An old Indian saying, "mink and muskrat bad friends," aptly describes the perpetual feud that exists between these two animals within the habitat they share. One would assume that the mink always wins hands down in such confrontations; however, in deep water a mature muskrat is a willing aggressor that can drown a full-grown mink.

There is evidence that sometimes the mink will hang by its jaw from birds in flight until the birds are brought down dead. Hartley Jackson, in his book *Mammals of Wisconsin,* describes a mallard with a large hole and blood stains on the upper left base of the neck, showing where a mink (identified by its tracks) had attacked the bird. All evidence, he says, clearly indicated that the mallard flew for many yards from open water with the mink dangling from its neck.

All in all, this svelte and sinuous animal is a voracious predator, although less bloodthirsty than the weasel. It may catch more than it needs but will store leftovers for future use. One such mink larder disclosed a super spread of thirteen freshly killed muskrats, two mallards, and one coot.

More agile on land than the otter, the mink hunts constantly. It can cover long reaches of shoreland in a night. No stone is left unturned as it rambles; it inspects every crevice or cranny for possible prey. In winter, it tunnels beneath the snow; in summer, it moves along rapidly in a nervous wandering walk or a bounding lope, hiding behind small obstacles, rising on its hind legs from time to time to peer about.

When under attack, the mink can slip into shelter in no time at all, but if cornered it is a formidable foe. This short-tempered fighter will claw, screech, hiss, and snarl, twisting its face in fury. Few animals have the nerve to attack it. The great horned owl, snowy owl, lynx, bobcat, wolf, and fox are known to be its enemies. Trappers in Louisiana report that alligators in the coastal marshes also take their toll. Within the weasel family, it is also preyed upon by the river otter and its own close kin, other mink. Enemy Number One is the trapper with his unflinching steel snares. When caught, this animal has been known to bite off its fettered foot or even bury itself, trap and all, in a desperate attempt to get away.

If injured, irritated, or excited, the mink resorts to chemical warfare, releasing a stream of fetid liquid from its scent glands. This musk is stronger

With beady black eyes, the mink peeks out of its den.

than that of the weasel or even the skunk, but luckily, the mink lacks the skunk's firing capacity. More often the musk is used as an inter-mink communication device rather than as a defense mechanism. Males at mating time become carried away with their stench-making. They spray at the slightest provocation — the older the mink and the nearer to mating season, the worse the smell. Fortunately for its neighbors, the mink spends much of its time in the water.

During mating season, mink are a promiscuous and feisty lot. Duels among competing males sometimes result in one or more dead mink. Much mink mate-swapping goes on before the male finally settles down with his last partner. As for the fickle female, her one litter may be the result of fertilization by different males or two ovulations more than a week apart.

Once the spraying, sparring, and spousing are over, gestation can extend from thirty-nine to seventy-six days due to delayed implantation. Most often the four to ten kits are born in fifty-one days. At birth, each is covered with white down and is about the size of a human's little finger. The adult mink, normally nasty, become devoted parents during the next eight or nine weeks. The kits nurse from their mother and, after their eyes open at five weeks. receive meat brought home by both parents. They soon want to venture outside the den and may be carried about by the scruff of the neck, or when in the water, on their parents' backs. Family hunting parties are organized when the kits grow larger. During these nightly expeditions, the young mink learn the value of thoroughness; they are taught to inspect every nook, cranny, hole, and brush pile for food, a practice they will pursue throughout their lives.

When it comes to fur coats, the most comely is mink. The wild mink pelt is usually a dark chocolate brown, with coarse guard hairs one to one and one-half inches long. Only a few white patches on the chin, throat, and belly interrupt its uniform color. The patches are larger on females, especially around the mammary glands. The underfur is thick and wavy, nearly two-thirds of an inch long. Like gold and diamonds, a coat made of mink pelts is a symbol of luxury recognized throughout the world.

There is much demand for wild mink, as it is durable and beautiful. Many factors, including color, condition, pelt size, and changing popularity, influence the price each pelt will bring. Female pelts are smaller and silkier; male pelts, however, are also desirable because their larger size reduces labor

The svelte and sinuous mink is seldom far from water.

costs. Prices at Seattle's Fur Exchange varied in 1973 from a low of $6 for small skins to $50 for large, quality pelts. Generally, the prime furs that bring the highest prices are from former residents of the Lower Yukon and Kuskokwim areas of Alaska. Between the price extremes, there are a number of variations in quality, color, and size.

It is a long way from the rugged lifestyle of the trapper to the elegant existence of the lady in mink. The trapper must be equipped with stamina, patience, and a thorough knowledge of this wily weasel. He must prevent his traps from being buried in the snow and has to brave winter hardships. There is a payoff for this rough life, however: the collective income received by mink trappers in Alaska, a prime area, often exceeds a million dollars a year. Of course, there are bad years when mink populations are low, and not all areas produce perfect wild pelts. For instance, an iron deficiency in the diet of wild mink in such areas as Oregon's Willamette Valley can result in poor-quality fur. These pelts, known as "cotton mink," are of little value.

The fur ranch is responsible for achieving stability and fine quality in mink pelt production. Because of this efficient production at least five million mink are raised on America's fur ranches yearly, a figure which represents roughly 40 percent of the market.

Although cool climates seem to be beneficial for raising these furbearers, proper nutrition and professional knowledge of selective breeding are the chief factors in achieving the finest-quality mink. Rich chocolates, pale beiges, silver-blues, lavenders, platinums, and even pale rose coats are the result of careful crossbreeding and mutations. Exotic names — Cerulean, Rovalia, Jasmine, Tourmaline, Diadem, and Azurene Violet — enhance the glamor of these furs, which vary greatly in price, depending on quality and current popularity.

The fur rancher is subject to the whims of the fashion world. Because of the many varieties of ranch mink, he must anticipate fashion trends by stocking breeders of the appropriate variety. An average pelt at auction in 1974 sold for about $22. At present, the most expensive is the Standard Ranch Mink, a luxurious, nearly black pelt. The best grades of female Ranch Mink pelts bring $24 each and up; for the larger male pelts, prices begin at $45 apiece. Once made into a full-length coat, a process which requires from 65 to 100 skins, the Standard Ranch model will cost from $3,000 to $7,000.

From man's point of view, the mink is both troublesome and helpful. On one hand, it raids henhouses and destroys game birds; on the other, it controls a variety of rodents, rabbits, and insects, and provides the most beautiful fur coat of all the small furbearers. Certainly, the mink's value as a fine predator and peltbearer tips the scale in its favor.

Marten *(Martes americana)*

Combine the cunning of a fox, the caution of a weasel, the voracity of a mink, the climbing ability of a raccoon, and you have a marten — the arboreal expert of the weasel tribe.

Scientifically known as *Martes americana,* this animal is also called the American sable for its lustrous fur, pine marten because of its habitat in pine forests and fondness for pine cone seeds, and rock marten for its love of high, rugged places. In appearance, it presents another combination: the body and ears of a housecat, the tail of a squirrel, and the reddish-brown coloration of a fox. In fact, on the ground it is sometimes mistaken for a red fox at first sight — a rare sight indeed, for like most of the mustelids, this animal is a fast mover.

Martes americana has lustrous, large eyes that shine brightly in its small, pointed face, one that is pleasant and alert in repose. It weighs up to four pounds with almost one-third of its twenty-four- to thirty-inch length a full, bushy tail that serves as a balance when it scampers through the trees. In addition, its five well-clawed toes, in winter cushioned with a growth of fur, ensure a good grip on life aloft.

The marten has anal glands, as well as an elongated scent gland under the belly skin, from which it leaves a secretion on the ground or on projecting branches for prospective mates. Though these scent marks must be renewed from time to time, studies on European martens reveal that branches bearing such seductive secretions keep their characteristic smell even after two weeks of exposure to wind and weather.

Along with its scents, the marten has a repertoire of sounds it can evoke — snarls, growls, squeaks, whines, hisses, and a special chuckle that the female uses as a love call at mating time.

Throughout most of the year, the marten spends its waking hours in the trees, forsaking them only during winter months. High in the piney boughs, it is only an orange-brown blur, flashing from branch to branch, as it pursues a passion for its favorite prey, the red squirrel. When deprived of that food, it will stoop to other diets: mice, chipmunks, pikas, rodents, other small mammals, birds, frogs, snakes, and when available, honey, pine cone seeds, and berries. (Blue-lipped martens have been found in Alaska — not from the cold, but from berries in season.) Mainly they are carnivorous; marten studies in Montana reveal that declines in their numbers closely follow a decrease in small mammal density.

The marten is less bloodthirsty than the weasel or the mink; it seldom kills more than it can eat. Nor is it as willing a swimmer; it will go long distances to avoid water, catching fish or frogs only if it can grab or splash them onto a bank from the water's edge. Like its kin, the marten is a ceaseless hunter. It wanders constantly, poking into holes and under bushes, always keeping a sharp eye on the trees overhead. When it spots possible prey aloft, it is up in a flash.

The marten has few enemies. Man, the trapper, is its most formidable foe, followed by the fisher, one of its own family. The great horned owl and other winged predators will attack the young. Because of its habit of hunting at night and hiding by day, the marten is less apt to encounter enemies. When it does, it is usually far too fast in the trees to be caught.

For habitat, the marten prefers mature evergreen forests, often at higher elevations. In winter, it forages for food, tunneling under the snow at 4,000-

In winter, the marten's well-clawed toes are cushioned with a growth of fur.

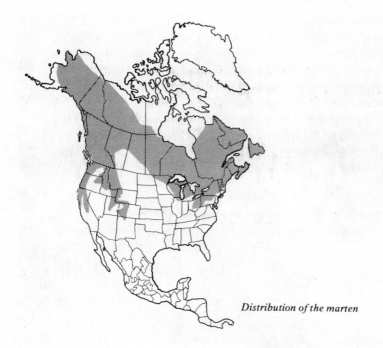

Distribution of the marten

to 7,000-foot altitudes. In summer, it may move higher and take to the trees or rocky areas well above the timberline.

At one time, the marten was found in most of the continent's coniferous forests. Today its range is greatly reduced — it is rarely seen in New England, only sometimes around the Great Lakes. It has been spotted in New York State and in the Adirondacks. In the Pacific Northwest states and in northwestern Canada, it is more common. Fortunate hikers and backpackers may catch a glimpse of this brown-coated carnivore in any of the high wilderness areas of Washington's North Cascades, in the Olympic or Mount Rainier national parks (where some are almost tame), along the upper elevations of the Blue and Wallowa mountains, or in the mountains of northern California. The marten is also found in coastal forests; some have been reported in the dense lowlands along the seashore. Inland, the vast primitive area of central Idaho also provides privacy and space for this freedom-loving animal. Throughout the coniferous forests of Canada, the marten has managed to hold on, in spite of the fact that it was for many years the main target of the fur trapper. The establishment of national parks, like Jasper Park in Alberta, has provided refuge.

When man moves in, the marten moves out. Even in the vast northwest forests, the population is small compared to the larger numbers of mink and weasel. Though Alaska's vast timbered areas still support large marten populations (about 6,000 pelts are taken annually), elsewhere in the Pacific Northwest it is less abundant. Pressure from many years of trapping and heavy logging in British Columbia has reduced the marten population and habitat. Reflecting the same trend, the Oregon Game Commission reports that it is rare in the northern Coast Range and cannot be considered abundant anywhere in the state. California asks wilderness travelers to report sightings of all three of its rare and protected mustelids: wolverine, fisher, and marten.

Perhaps as improved forestry methods perpetuate a suitable habitat for the marten, restocking the species will yield a more viable population. This has been done twice in Michigan, but apparently without success. During the winters of 1955-57 and again in 1968-70 a total of 128 martens were released in the forests of Michigan's Upper Peninsula. Since these forests had matured to the point where they would support marten, wildlife officials had high hopes for restoring a native animal. However, there are no signs of success from either transplant — the martens apparently scattered widely upon release. The only one found so far was hit by a car some 150 miles from the release point.

If successful, a policy of restocking the marten would aid man, for in addition to its role as a rodent predator, the marten has a pelt which is durable and of high quality. Indeed, the name *martre*, meaning sable, indicates its relationship to the valuable Russian fur from Siberia. Soft and fluffy, the pelt of *Martes americana* varies in color from blond to a near black. It may be somewhat grizzled in pelts taken from Alaska or nearly black in those from Labrador. It is generally a warm, lustrous brown, blending to lighter pale orange underparts. The fur is longer than mink, softened with a silky undercoat, with glossy guard hairs on top. Ideal as trim on collars and cuffs, about 10,000 pelts are harvested in the United States each year. Canada harvests more than 60,000 annually, most from Quebec and Ontario. The pelts bring an average price of $14. Those trapped in Alaska and northern Canada normally bring higher prices than furs from Washington's Cascades or from the coast. In Washington, about 230 martens are harvested yearly; in Idaho, about 1,100 are taken in alternate years, a longer interval that permits protection of the species. Pelts at auction in Seattle bring from $5 to $40 apiece, depending upon color and size.

Due to the marten's native curiosity, it is probably the easiest of the weasels to trap. In its encounter with men, inquisitiveness often overcomes caution, and despite the trap awaiting it, the marten cannot resist the temptation to investigate something new. Any bright, shiny, or tinkly object will attract these creatures, as will a variety of scents, including cheap perfume. Of course, meat or fish will do a first-class job. Marten trapping does have its drawbacks, however. Trappers find martens hard to catch in winter, due to their habit of traveling and foraging under the deep snow. Pelts of martens trapped in deep or crusted snow are often of poor quality, damaged by constant contact with their tunnel walls.

Desirable as it may be for collars and cuffs, the marten's fur is more attractive on its original owner. Each July, the male marten, adorned in fluffy brown courting pelage, leaves a scent from his powerful musk glands on tree trunks, logs, and rocks. When the female picks up this scent, she begins her coquettish chuckling and courtship ensues. Both males and females, otherwise quite hostile toward each other, may have several mates during this season. The results of these encounters — three or four fuzzy yellow young — are born some nine months later in late March or early April.

At birth the little martens weigh only one-half ounce. After six weeks, their eyes open and they are introduced to solid food. Until midsummer they remain with their mother in the nest, frolicking and squeaking in mock warfare. The young martens are as frisky as the squirrels they will pursue as adults. They scramble and roughhouse all over the den, making small, savage squeals and squeaks. Life for them becomes more serious and intense as summer passes; hunting exercises begin and the young learn to fend for themselves. As the days shorten into fall, they are ready for a lifetime of squirrel chasing through the forests.

Fisher *(Martes pennanti)*

In the pure white silence of the winter forest, a snowshoe hare searches for tidbits to munch on. As it samples the twigs of hardwood shrubs, it passes under a sweep of low-hanging pine branches. Suddenly, the snowy setting is split by a black flash from the branches overhead, and the stillness is rent by the bleat of a dying hare. It has just lost out in a confrontation with *Martes pennanti*, the deadly fisher.

The fisher is as aggressive and accurate a predator as can be found. It can lick a coyote, bobcat, fox, or even a deer if the snow is deep enough. It is extremely quick — the fastest of all tree-traveling mammals. Though a marten may be able to run rings around a fast squirrel, a fisher can run rings around a marten — which it often does, as martens are included on its list of frequent foods.

Physically, the fisher looks like an oversized marten, so much so that the Chippewa Indian named it *tha-cho,* or large marten. The fisher body is typically weasel shaped, long and sinuous, with short, sturdy legs. However, the head, with small eyes and prominently pointed muzzle, is more weasellike than that of its marten relative. Though it has the family musk glands, the fisher's odor is not paticularly offensive.

Size and color most clearly distinguish the fisher from the marten. The fisher is nearly three times heavier. Mature males can weigh twelve pounds and measure over three feet in length; females are half as large. (So far, the weight record is twenty pounds for a fisher found in 1964.) Differing from its brown-red relative, the fisher's darker fur varies from ashy gray to almost black. It is sometimes frosted on top of the head, neck, and shoulders.

Martes pennanti has a variety of names: black fox, black cat, pekan (from French Canadian), Pennant's cat (from an eighteenth-century naturalist), and fisher marten. Why it is called fisher remains a mystery — fish are a very minor item in its diet. In their journal, Lewis and Clark described the many-faceted fisher: "The black fox . . . the fisher . . . is found in the woody country bordering on the coast. How it should have acquired this appellation, it is difficult to imagine, as it certainly does not prey upon fish. These animals are extremely strong and active, and admirably expert in climbing; this they perform with the greatest ease, and bound from tree to tree in pursuit of the squirrel or raccoon, their most usual food. Their color is jetty black, excepting a small white spot upon the breast; the body is long, the legs are short, resembling those of the ordinary turn-spit dog. The tail is remarkably long, not differing in other particulars from that of the ordinary fox." With all due respect to the explorers, close observation has proven that the fisher is more slender than a fox; it also has rounded, not pointed ears.

Today the fisher is relatively rare. Although never numerous, its population has been diminished by logging, forest fires, and trapping. The fisher originally wandered through the northern coniferous forests from coast to coast, in the east as far south as the mountains of Virginia and Tennessee. As the logger and farmer cleared the land, this retiring animal lost the dense forest cover it needed for habitat. Then, too, came the trapper, who easily snared the inquisitive fisher for its fur, which at the turn of the century, was in great demand. (The 1920s brought an average price of $85 per pelt in Canada, with one exceptional pelt selling for $345.) By the 1930s, the fisher

The fisher body is typically weasel shaped.

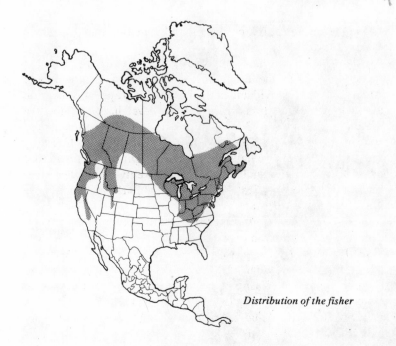

Distribution of the fisher

was all but gone in the United States. Only small populations held out in Maine, the White and Adirondack mountains, northern Minnesota, and California (where only two were taken in 1931).

Because of this drastic decrease, many states closed the trapping season on fishers, and Canada began to more closely monitor its fisher harvests — two actions which probably saved the animal from extinction.

Then the fisher began a slow comeback. Over the years, the northern forests that had been overcut and overburned during the 1920s slowly began to grow back, once again forming suitable habitat. As a result, there has been a rise in the number of these animals within the past twenty years. New York, Maine, and New Hampshire have recorded enough fishers to open limited trapping seasons. Minnesota has noted more fishers since the 1940s; a large and stable population now dwells in that state's northern woodlands. In both Minnesota and Michigan, where fisher trapping is closed, fishers are caught in snares set for other animals (fox or coyote) and sometimes sold at black market prices out of state.

In the Pacific Northwest, the rare fisher is also returning. Here, it originally wandered through the Blue, Cascade, Wallowa, Siskiyou, and coastal mountains, but man's civilizing activities — plus traps, poisons, fire, and the axe — cut its population to the danger level in the 1940s. To counteract the drop, the Oregon Game Commission in 1961 transplanted twenty-four fishers from British Columbia to the Wallowa and Cascade-Siskiyou ranges. Since then, there have been enough sightings to prove that the fisher is still around. Between 1955 and 1972, twenty-one fishers were recorded in and around Oregon's Crater Lake National Park, and eight more were sighted in other parts of the state.

Washington and northern California are also reporting more fishers, although the picture in Washington is less bright. Of the nine sightings in the past five years in this state, eight were on the Olympic Peninsula, one in North Cascades National Park. Early in 1955, one fisher was identified in Okanogan County in eastern Washington. In the northwestern corner of California, many more have been seen — fifty-seven between 1962 and 1973, most of them along the Trinity and Klamath rivers. Washington, Oregon, and California have declared the fisher a protected species. In Idaho, it is listed as a "former resident." British Columbia, with its abundant wilderness, still has a viable fisher population.

Remote areas, especially dense conifer forests at 3,500 to 7,000 feet, provide the choicest fisher habitat. These are generally lower elevations than those occupied by the high-living marten and wolverine; however, marten-fisher ranges do overlap and competition for food can limit the population growth of these species. In these wild areas, the fisher establishes a territory of about ten square miles. Over a period of several days, it will make its solitary rounds in search of food, moving from one temporary shelter in a hollow tree or log to another. A stealthy predator, it normally hunts by night, though in the leaner midwinter months it will forage in daylight. Small mammals — squirrels, rabbits, hares, marmots, beavers, wood rats, mice, raccoons — are its chosen prey, followed by birds, frogs, and occasional fish. In a pinch, it will eat nuts, berries, or even carrion taken from traps.

The fisher also has a taste for porcupine. It is the only predator to successfully reduce porcupine populations, thus befriending itself to the lumberman, who frequently must contend with the damage done by these tree-girdling animals. Though it is a popular myth that the fisher bests the prickly porky by flipping it over and biting into the throat or belly, observations of fishers in the wild made by Malcolm Coulter indicate that this is untrue. Coulter reports that the fisher attacks the porcupine head-on, its teeth and claws scratching at the porky's face, while it jumps out of the way to avoid the tail. As the porky weakens, the fisher begins feeding either at the belly or the head. Little is left when the meal is finished, except a few scattered quills.

The porcupine's quills, which are so disastrous and sometimes fatal to other animals, do not harm the fisher. Analysis of dead fishers with partially dissolved quills lodged in the skin, stomach, or muscles shows little inflammation or infection. Although there is no explanation for this resistance, it is most certainly important to the fisher's success against the porcupine.

Paradoxically, it takes the lightning speed of the fisher to control one of the slowest-moving mammals in North America. With the drastic decrease of fishers in the 1920s, the porky population began to proliferate. Tree damage reached serious proportions in New York, Wisconsin, and Michigan. In one area, the porcupine density rose to between thirty and sixty per square mile. In order to provide an ecological solution to the problem, and to restore a native animal to its habitat, a series of fisher transplants were initiated.

In 1947, Nova Scotia reintroduced fishers and now has a viable population. The Oregon transplant, already mentioned, occurred in 1961 and probably accounts for the fisher's success in that state. Montana received 36 fishers from British Columbia in 1959 and transplanted these animals into its western spruce-fir forests. Wisconsin brought a total of 120 fishers into the hardwood and conifer stands of Nicolet (1956-60) and Chequamegon (1966) national forests. Michigan, which had reported in 1928 that "there is no chance they will ever come back," transplanted 61 fishers from Minnesota to the Ottawa National Forest of the Upper Peninsula (1961-63). The results are heartening. Fishers have reproduced, particularly in the Great Lakes region. In some areas, there is also evidence that the porcupine has met its match once again. After transplant, Michigan porcupine numbers dropped over the next ten years, decreasing in one spot from 36 to 9 per square mile. In 1954, Forest County, Wisconsin highway crews counted 208 porkies; in 1965 along

As a fighter, the fisher has no peer.

the same area there were only 25. Even damage to highway signs was reduced in this county — a twenty-five-mile stretch of road on which thirty signs were once replaced (at forty dollars each) because of the porkies' penchant for pine signs!

Today Joel Anderson of Gustavus Adolphus College in Minnesota is monitoring the fisher's habits and movements. Using radio tracking equipment and aerial observations, he and two students are investigating population data, movements, and food habits. The study emphasizes that the fisher's predatory ability and opportunistic nature have made it important to nearly all ecological roles and populations of the dense forest habitat.

Each April, the female fisher gives birth to her young, and within a few days is ready to mate again. Delayed implantation extends the gestation period to fifty weeks, until the following April, when one to five (usually three) young are born in the shelter of a hollow tree. At seven weeks, the little fishers' eyes open. They are fed by their mother. Carrying food in her mouth, she scurries up and down the tree like a squirrel. Three months later, they begin to forage with her. When the family separates in late fall, the young fishers' education is complete.

As a fighter, the fisher has no peer. Equipped with speed, a vicious temper, an ability to leap as far as sixteen feet in one prodigious bound, and complete lack of fear, it can take on almost any animal. Bobcats, coyotes, or dogs are no match for its ferocity. Larger carnivores cannot equal its speed in the trees. On the ground, where it spends most of its time, all of the typical weasel defenses are put to use when the fisher is threatened: bared fangs, arched back, a furious fit of snarls, shrieks, and hisses — with a final fusillade of disagreeable musk. If startled coming headfirst down a tree, the fisher will beat its forepaws against the trunk while hanging on with its hind feet, a performance that serves either as a challenge to an intruder or as a warning to the young of an enemy approach.

With such a reputation for ferocity, what kind of a pet does the fisher make? Newborn fishers can be an all-consuming chore. In Watersmeet, Michigan, Roger Powell is studying metabolic rates in fishers. Hand-raised fishers are important to his study for obtaining data on a treadmill. He has thus raised ThaCho and Uskool since they were kits. Powell explains that they are born in an almost fetal state (150-200 grams), only slightly furred with eyes and ears tightly closed. Feeding schedules at all hours, fear of dehydration from diarrhea, constant changing of diet as they grow are just a few of the trials of Powell's fisher fatherhood. Still, he says he will miss the day when his study is finished and they begin their gradual return to the wild.

Glenn Maxham, a filmmaker from Duluth, Minnesota, raised a fisher for several years. Suzie, as she was called, was found in the wild while still very young. She grew up in a pen and roamed about within the confines of the Maxham homestead. "She was a very loving little creature," he recalled in an interview, "constantly on the go, as if she'd been wound up like a watch.

Unless sleeping, she was never quiet. She loved to jump and would sometimes sail half way across the room into my arms. She'd also drive the birds mad, running up a tree trunk, out on the limb, sometimes upside down like a sloth. At other times, she'd climb up a hollow cedar tree out in the yard. I'd stand back about eight feet, and she'd leap across into my arms, never clawing me, and then run down my body headfirst and do it all over again. She was a totally delightful animal with actions much like a kitten." Maxham feels the fisher's ferocity is greatly overplayed.

As Suzie grew, she was moved into the garage and allowed to come and go, in order to ease herself back into her natural state. "Sometimes she'd go for a week and come back, go for two weeks and come back," recalls Maxham. "She went for increasingly long periods of time, and towards the last she really didn't want me to pick her up anymore. Then she was gone for three weeks during which there was a terrific snowstorm, and I figured maybe she was lost. But one Sunday morning my son found Suzie in the garage. I went out there, and sure enough there she was, climbing around on the rafters overhead. When she came down and over to my feet, I picked her up and loved her — I'd always hold her up on my neck and nuzzle her. Then I put her back down, went into the house. That's the last I saw of her."

Apart from rare instances such as these, man has become the only predator the fisher has to fear. He seems to possess an inexhaustible hunger for this elegant animal's fur. Long and glossy, with a fine layer of silky underfur for insulation, the fisher's pelt has been described by Peter Matthiessen as "individually, except for rare strains of the red fox, the most valuable of all North American land species" (a comparison which excludes the sea otter). Due to their scarcity nowadays, only 8,000 or 9,000 fishers are trapped in North America each year, a relatively small number when compared to the 200,000 mink taken in Louisiana in one year alone. The full-length fisher fur coat, which is becoming more popular, now costs between $10,000 and $15,000. The pelts sell at Canadian auction for an average of $48 each; larger specimens with dark, uniform coloration can bring up to $55. Since the fisher, like the marten, responds poorly to captivity, its future as a commercial species is highly doubtful.

The fisher is of great value to man because of its fine pelt and its role as a rodent predator. Although relatively scarce, it is hoped this rugged individualist of the weasel family will continue to have a fighting chance.

BADGER

(page 73)

The bulldozing badger is the earthmover of the weasel family.

BLACK-FOOTED FERRET (page 80)

The black-footed ferret—rarest North American mammal.

In keeping with its covert nature, the ferret hides behind a mask.

Curious little ferrets take a peek around a prairie dog town.

Black-footed ferrets at play.

FISHER *(page 39)*

The fleet-footed fisher is the
fastest tree-traveling mammal.

Long and glossy, the elegant fisher's fur
is considered one of the most valuable.

53

MARTEN *(page 33)*

**Bright eyed and bushy tailed, the
marten is the arboreal expert.**

The marten catches fish only if it can grab or splash them onto a bank from the water's edge.

High in the piney boughs, the marten surveys its realm.

MINK   *(page 25)*

The svelte and sinuous mink is a voracious predator.

A bundle of curious energy, the mink is seldom still.

OTTER   *(pages 106, 114)*

A fine flare of whiskers aids the river otter in his search for food.

The fun-loving and sociable river otter often plays on pontoons and docks.

The sea otter is a marine-going member of the weasel tribe.

SKUNK   *(pages 92, 99, 104)*

A dryland denizen, the hognosed skunk is one of four kinds of North American skunk.

LONG-TAILED WEASEL   *(page 15)*

**Tooth for tooth and ounce for ounce, the weasel is the
fiercest and most efficient predator in the mammal world.**

SHORT-TAILED WEASEL   *(page 15)*

The short-tailed weasel, commonly called the ermine, in its summer coat.

LEAST WEASEL   *(page 15)*

The two-ounce least weasel is the tiniest carnivore in the world.

WOLVERINE *(page 66)*

Unpredictable, vengeful, solitary, there is nothing halfway about the wolverine.

Bearlike, the wolverine lumbers through the snow.

Wolverine *(Gulo gulo)*

Although the fisher may be the individualist of the weasel family, the wolverine is the true eccentric.

Unpredictable, vengeful, solitary, there is nothing halfway about the wolverine. It carries all the weasel family traits to extremes. If the fisher is rarely seen, the wolverine is almost *never* seen; if the mink appears to be constantly hungry, its requirements are nothing when likened to the appetite of this glutton. Even the hisses and snarls of a fighting marten sound like sweet nothings when compared with the wolverine, which probably has the nastiest disposition in the whole family. As a result, this animal has earned a variety of nicknames — glutton or *glouton* in French Canada, *carcajou* (Indian for evil spirit), Indian devil, mountain devil, and skunk bear, because it smells like a skunk, looks like a bear, and has the short temper of both. Many of its nicknames just cannot be printed.

In addition to being the black sheep of the family, the wolverine is also the ugly duckling. The long, sinewy grace of its smaller relatives seems to have been fattened and flattened, resulting in a shaggy, shuffling, brown-furred animal with yellowish bands extending along its squat body and rump. There may also be light markings on the head and throat. It usually weighs somewhere between twenty and fifty pounds and measures three to three and one-half feet long, the largest land-going member of the weasel tribe. For its size, this short, bowlegged scrapper is the strongest of all North American mammals.

Despite its ungainly appearance, the wolverine is surprisingly agile and a very good climber. Its outsized paws, which can measure as much as four inches across, are tipped by a well-developed set of strong claws. With them it can rip apart anything from beaver houses to trappers' caches and drag heavy kills several miles. It has also been known to climb trees or high boulders to leap upon its prey. One eighteenth-century naturalist, Thomas Pennant, described this wolverine habit: "By a wonderful sagacity, it will ascend a tree, and fling from the boughs a species of moss which elks and rains [reindeer] are very fond of; and when those animals come beneath to feed on it, will fall on them and destroy them; or, like the lynx, it ascends to the boughs of trees, and falls on the deer which casually pass beneath it, and adheres till they fall down with fatigue." Although there is evidence that wolverines do kill Dall sheep in this manner, the description of "flinging moss" only illustrates one of many unclear and rumored traits of this elusive animal. Since little is known about the wolverine's lifestyle, it probably is credited with more than it deserves.

Some facts are known, however. The wolverine has a well-earned reputation for being incredibly voracious and vindictive. Simply speaking, it is a very hungry beast, equipped with a highly efficient digestive system which quickly disposes of immense quantities of food. Thus, it is perpetually hungry. *Gulo,* its generic name, is derived from the Latin meaning "gullet." Because its former specific name was *luscus,* meaning "half-blind," it was generally assumed that the wolverine had bad eyesight. This misnomer originated because the first captured specimen had accidentally lost an eye.

Until the nineteenth century, many thought the wolverine was a bear. Though it has been considered a plantigrade animal like the bear, close observation in zoos has proved that it walks mainly on its toes like most of the weasels.

Gulo gulo will eat anything it can subdue, although much of its diet consists of carrion which it can pick on at its leisure. Though its dietary range extends from mouse to moose, of these it usually subsists on mice,

A shaggy, shuffling wolverine on the prowl.

chipmunks, ground squirrels, ptarmigan, and marmots. When it sees another animal having a good feed, it can become highly incensed and, livid with greed, move in on the scene. Even grizzlies and cougars have been driven from their kills by this nasty animal.

In the remote wilderness, the wolverine hunts at all hours and in all seasons, moving along with a sort of hunchbacked lope. Birds, fish, amphibians, mammals, even berries are all part of its diet. Should a large animal such as a moose or caribou bog down in the snow, its fate is sealed if the wolverine happens along. Only the porcupine merits its respect, for wolverines have been found dead with their mouths, throats, stomach walls, or intestines pierced by its barbed quills.

The little-known life history of the wolverine begins with a litter of one to five (usually two or three) born between January and April in an improvised snow cave or sheltered cranny. At birth, the woolly young are covered with soft cream-colored fur. For eight or nine weeks, they are nursed and protected by their mother as they grow. No one is certain, but there is some evidence that male wolverines visit the dens and may play a role in rearing the young. However, these visits could also be made in hopes of a free meal or female affection. By fall, the brown-coated young wolverines are two-thirds grown and ready to make their own way in the wilderness. They will keep to themselves as adults until mating season, which occurs between May and July.

Few North American animals are surrounded by such an aura of myth as this mustelid. Trappers have contributed much to the lore, and as the tales get taller, it becomes more difficult to separate fact from fancy. All agree, however, that the wolverine can play havoc with humans. This canny beast will mercilessly follow a trap line, eat any furbearers already caught, and spring all other traps. It has even been known to carry off the trap and bury it some distance away. Some trappers have been forced to move out of a territory entirely because of the wolverine's relentless raids. In its search for food, the wolverine will break into cabins and tear everything to shreds. What it cannot eat or break, it sprays with its musk. It smashes furniture, eats snowshoes, fouls bedding, and rips apart doors and windows. Canned goods, pots, pans, and dishes are scattered throughout the woods as if from sheer deviltry. All in all, the wolverine is what you might call a real home wrecker.

When not bedeviling the trapper, the wolverine is rarely seen or captured. Having a very low tolerance for civilization, it requires extensive wilderness above the 4,000-foot level for comfortable habitat. Although never numerous in the United States, it was once found in the woods and mountains across the continent as far south as Pennsylvania. Today the wolverine still wanders throughout Alaska and across the subarctic forests of northern Canada and Eurasia, but in lower latitudes it has declined.

Even in Michigan, the Wolverine State, it is gone. (Some Michiganders deny that the wolverine ever was a resident of their state; they say the nickname evolved from the many wolverine pelts brought into Michigan for sale by early fur traders from Canada.) After the 1920s, the wolverine was rarely seen in the Rockies or high wilderness areas of the Pacific Northwest — that is, up until the 1960s, when a few sightings began to trickle in. The wily wolverine was not quite ready to give up yet.

In Washington State between 1930 and 1960, there was only one confirmed report of a wolverine. Then came an unexplained increase: in 1963, a wolverine was shot in a Yakima County apple orchard; the following year an adult male was trapped on top of a mountain in Douglas County. (In typical wolverine style, it had broken loose and dragged the trap for several miles.) Since then, there have been at least six more animals identified in the high mountains of the north central Cascades, making the wolverine one of the few rare mammals to show a marked increase in the state.

In Oregon, the story is similar. Although early records show that wolverines were once present in small numbers in Oregon's Cascades, only

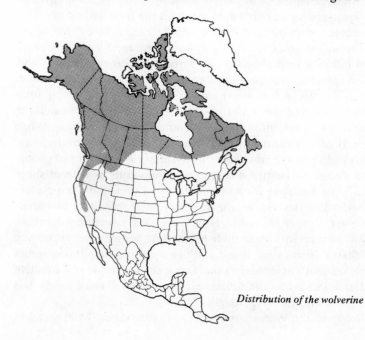

Distribution of the wolverine

Rarely seen or captured, this short bowlegged scrapper, a wolverine, was found at Auke Bay, near Juneau.

one was sighted between 1912 and 1965. Since that time, seventeen have been reliably identified or unintentionally taken in traps. Most of these were found in the Three Sisters Wilderness Area, along the eastern slopes of Mount Hood, and in the Wallowa Mountains of the northeastern part of the state. Another wolverine was photographed shuffling along the high desert ridges of Steens Mountain in southeastern Oregon.

Even as far south as California, the wolverine is making a comeback. There are some sparse old records of these animals in and near Sequoia and Yosemite national parks. Since 1966, however, the reports are more frequent — twelve wandering wolverines in the Siskiyou and Salmon mountains of northern California.

In the Idaho mountains, a few wolverines are now seen after an absence of over fourteen years. Others have been known to turn up in Utah, Colorado, and western Wyoming. Some rare wanderers have strayed south from Canada into the Dakotas, one reported as far south as Iowa. Minnesota's northern forests also harbor this large mustelid. Filmmaker Glenn Maxham, in an article in *The Minnesota Volunteer*, has listed seven verified reports of wolverines in that state since 1967.

Montana may have the highest wolverine population in the "Lower 48." As elsewhere in the Rocky Mountain area, the wolverine nearly disappeared in the 1920s. However, slowly but surely, it has reestablished itself in Montana to the point where fur trappers have brought in over 200 wolverine pelts within the past ten years. In northwestern Montana, the University of Idaho is now conducting a four-year project to study radio-collared wolverines, hoping to answer many questions about this mysterious animal's habits, diet, and movements.

What has caused the increase? Dr. Charles Yocom of California State University has watched the wolverines' movements along the coastal states since 1953 and finds two reasons that may account for the change. According to the data compiled, the wolverine seems to be moving south from British Columbia, slowly returning to its old haunts in Washington, Oregon, and California. (The wide-ranging male wolverine apparently makes the first move, since many of those identified have been adult males. In time, the females follow and successful reproduction occurs.) It is also possible that small breeding populations did remain in remote areas and, increasing over the past thirty years, are now finally spreading out into former ranges. To aid in its comeback, the wolverine is completely protected in California, Washington, Idaho, Oregon, Colorado, and Wyoming. It receives no legal classification in Iowa, North Dakota, South Dakota, or Utah. In Montana and Minnesota it may be killed at any time.

The wolverine's fur, glossy and somewhat stiff, is too bulky and hard to find to be used as a coat or jacket. It is, however, frost-free, and thus in great demand as trim for parka hoods. Over 1,200 wolverines were trapped in Canada during 1973-74, most of these from the Yukon Territory and British Columbia, bringing an average price of $85 per pelt. The Seattle Fur Exchange, indicating a strong demand for this fur, received prices in 1973 ranging from $40 to $55 for dark pelts and up to $130 for very pale skins.

Eskimos call the wolverine *kee-wa-har-kess*, the Evil One, because of its cunning plundering of trap lines. Its body, according to legend, houses the soul of a great hunter whose only pleasure is to plague hunters until they join his company of the damned. Whatever the wolverine's role, with luck this rare beast will remain with us, haunting the high wilderness and bedeviling the trapper with its wicked ways.

Badger *(Taxidea taxus)*

Sod, sand, or shale, the badger digs it all. Broad-shouldered and tough, the squat, chunky badger is the earthmover of the weasel family.

Few animals are more ungainly than the badger, except perhaps the wolverine. At least the wolverine carries a mystique of tall tales and high, remote places with its name. The lowly badger, on the other hand, must settle for a more earthy existence digging in dry flatlands, maligned by ranchers and farmers for its burrowing habits. In appearance, this animal is short, heavy-bodied, wide, and flattened; bowlegged, pigeon-toed, and underslung. *Taxidea taxus* — no matter how you glamorize it — will never win a beauty contest.

Distinctive markings run in a white stripe from the badger's slightly upturned nose over its wide head, while white crescents behind each eye offset its dark face. On its back it wears a coat of many intermixed colors that produces an overall yellow-grizzled-gray effect. This grizzled fur drapes over a twenty-five-to thirty-inch body that can weigh from fifteen to twenty-five pounds at maturity. Short legs lift the whole shaggy mass only about nine inches off the ground. This proximity to the ground is fitting, for the badger is basically a down-to-earth fellow.

"They burrow in hard grounds with surprising ease and dexterity," wrote Lewis and Clark when they encountered the badger, "and will cover themselves in a very few moments." This disappearing act is accomplished with the help of five long fixed nails on each foot. These claws normally extend two inches and are kept clean and sharp at all times. They, with the help of powerful muscles and an aggressive disposition, can create tunnels in no time, with dirt showering in all directions. So well ingrained is this deep urge to dig that there is one report of a pair of badgers who managed to buckle the concrete on an airport runway.

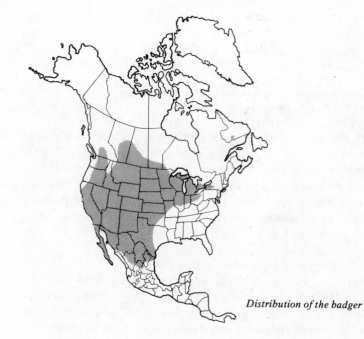

Distribution of the badger

The badger doesn't dig just for the sheer joy of moving earth. On the contrary, its whole life is dependent upon the burrows and tunnels it makes. Food is obtained by shoveling for ground squirrels, gophers, mice, and other burrowing animals. Shelter is made for either a brief rest in a burrow or more permanent housing when a prospective mother badger fashions an underground breeding den. The badger will also dig to bury its feces. Most important, when threatened, the badger can escape underground in a flash, plugging the hole behind it. All of these badger holes — whatever their purposes — are a pain to the rancher. They cause a hazard to horses and cattle and can even undermine irrigation ditches. However, as with other mustelids, this occasional damage is more than offset by the constant reduction of harmful rodents that the badger tirelessly pursues.

Badgers are found in dry open country throughout the western half of the United States from Mexico to Canada. In recent years, there has been some evidence that the badger is extending its range eastward. It has been found in New York and New England. Two as yet unproven reasons may explain this "migration": either these are badgers raised commercially and released when pelt prices dropped, or they may be moving in response to logging operations that encourage the rodent population on which badgers like to feed. When the natural forest is removed for agriculture, the crumbly soil made by tilling is most attractive to the bulldozing badger.

Dry as the badger may like its habitat, on occasion it has been known to swim. One was sighted crossing Devils Lake in North Dakota, another swimming with apparent ease in Oregon's Malheur Lake.

Ground squirrels, chipmunks, gophers, even poisonous snakes are taken by the badger in the dry, light-soiled sagebrush country where it lives. For variety, it also adds rabbits, birds, eggs, lizards, insects, snails, honeybee larvae, and carrion to its menu. Extra food may be buried or brought into a burrow for a few days of feasting.

Hunting mostly between dusk and dawn, the badger may be spotted along the highways of the dry eastern side of the Cascades in Washington and Oregon and throughout the lower elevations of the western and prairie states. Large, freshly dug elliptical burrows, eight to twelve inches wide, or mounds of dirt on open rangeland attest to its presence. Underground, it lies in wait for ground squirrels or reopens abandoned burrows to see if there are any unsuspecting residents to be preyed upon.

In Utah a badger-ground squirrel study uncovered some of the badger's predatory strategy. Nesting ground squirrels in this area had dug many burrows, each with a main entrance and additional entrances. The badger, attracted by signs that the little squirrels sometimes clustered outside these entrances in the sun, plugged up the accessory entrances and dug into the main tunnel after its prey.

In Idaho the badger is widely distributed, at least throughout the southern half of the state, but in Washington, as in other parts of the West, its numbers have declined due to poison campaigns instituted against the coyote. According to trapping records, as many badgers as coyotes have been poisoned in some years along the Snake River. Nationwide, in 1963 when 1080 poison was in use, U.S. Fish and Wildlife figures included 7,000 badgers among the innocent victims of the war against the coyote.

In mountainous British Columbia the badger is even more scarce. Limited to the prairies and open forest in the southern part of the province, it is a protected species. Farther north to Alaska, the badger is absent.

Perhaps it is lucky that the badger's pelt is not in fashion, for it is not heavily trapped. Its hair can be gray at the base, blending to white, then black, and ending in a silvery tip. Though the guard hairs were popular for quality shaving brushes and as lining or trim for ladies' coats, they are no longer of economic value. In 1973-74, 5,000 were trapped in Canada, most from the dry plains of Saskatchewan. The pelts sold for an average price of twenty-one dollars each.

In autumn, the usually lone badger begins a search for its mate, spreading a musky scent from its abdominal glands as an invitation. After mating, the animals separate, fatten up, and dig dens for a winter sleep. This seasonal snooze occurs in the cold northerly ranges, but is unnecessary in lower latitudes. It is not true hibernation; the badgers will be up and about if there is a temporary warm spell but back to sleep when temperatures drop. With the supreme practicality of nature, the badger's inactive season coincides with the hibernation of the ground squirrel, its favorite food.

About mid-February, the embryo implants on the female badger's uterine wall and development continues. One to five badger babies are born some six weeks later, after a gestation of 183 to 265 days. They are born in a breeding den — a more spacious home than the temporary burrow. The dens measure from two to five feet in length and are located at the end of a tunnel that may

The badger digs in.

be thirty feet long. The little badgers' eyes open a month or six weeks after birth. As they grow, they may leave the den to sun themselves outside the burrow door, but their mother promptly herds them back inside if an intruder appears. Two-thirds grown by late summer, they are learning to swim, hunt, and above all, dig. Autumn finds them independent — as well as determined and fearsome — antagonists whenever necessary.

Never badger a badger — this is one tough animal. Though an occasional bobcat or coyote may attempt an attack, it will usually fail. The badger has murderous front claws, sharp teeth, and that secret mustelid weapon, strong musk. Furthermore, its low-slung design helps to protect a vulnerable throat and belly, and its loose skin makes it almost impossible to grasp. Once released, it is underground in a matter of seconds. If unable to dig, the badger at bay will not hesitate to charge man or beast.

An in-family fight between two male badgers is said to be something to remember. One Idaho writer described such a performance: "They engage in combat with such deadly fury that a human being can approach and kick them and they will remain unaware or wholly indifferent to his presence; and now and then they get their jaws locked in a death grip and die together. A badger is a creature of such enormous vitality that often one shot through with a rifle and carried all day behind a saddle will crawl off when thrown to the earth."

These animals are also difficult to catch and keep. Badgers in steel traps often dig themselves in so well that a man cannot pull them loose with the trap chain. There is one account of a captured badger that broke out of its heavy wire cage in a laboratory. For the better part of a night, it searched for an exit, moving two large storage cabinets from their place against the wall (it took four men to replace them later). It upset a variety of chemicals and finally ate its way to freedom through the wood panels of an outside door.

Fierce as its reputation may be, the badger has been known to cooperate with other animals. Occasionally a fox and a badger will share a den, an arrangement that seems to last as long as convenience dictates. There are also records of cooperative hunting between coyote and badger. In a joint effort, the badger will flush a hare from a brush hole or a prairie dog from a burrow. As the animal flees, it is ambushed by the waiting coyote, and both animals share the kill.

One of the most fascinating accounts of badger behavior appeared in *The Murrelet*, written by a woman who kept a badger in her home in Chelan County, Washington, for two months. The author, Mary Louise Perry, describes the badger as a friendly animal. She could pick it up by the nape of the neck, the front legs, or the loose hide on its back. When she washed its face and feet, the badger licked the soapsuds from its chin with apparent relish or gently gnawed her knuckles. Though it tolerated brushing of its coat, she noted that it seemed to prefer the feel of the bristles on its teeth!

The captive badger's table habits reflected a great love for various foods. She wrote: "When raw meat was presented, he became very excited and, eyeing me distrustfully, seized it and tried to hide it." Soon it was also demonstrating its urge to dig: "When I first took him out for an airing, he 'heeled' like a devoted dog, but on later expeditions he spent most of the time appraising the ground for burrowing. Nearing the vegetable garden, he usually made a wild dash and started digging furiously."

Whenever the badger sensed that it would be taken away from a digging site, it wedged its head into the hole and plowed through the ground at a furious speed. This digging reached its extreme when it began excavating the concrete basement floor. Whenever the badger found a flaw in the concrete, it picked out little pebbles until it could get a claw in and jerk out a section.

Attempts at discipline were met with hisses. "The badger did not seem to understand the emotions of anger or affection that the tones of my voice revealed, although he occasionally responded to his name (Elmer) by stopping whatever activity he was engaged in and looking for the source of my voice." The badger's own feelings, however, were clearly expressed: fear and displeasure by hoarse breathing, hissing, or piglike grunts; pain and anger with high-pitched grunts, yaps, and squeals. When excited, it bobbed up and down on its hind legs, wagging its head with open mouth. Sometimes, in its bobbing efforts, it would fall over backwards.

Elmer also became quite irritable when confined or restrained from moving. In an automobile, he tore around in a fury, breathing noisily, grunting and ripping at the upholstery with his long claws. All in all, the badger is not what you'd call the perfect household pet.

The author concluded that although the badger was quite tractable, attractive, playful, and healthy, its excitable nature created problems. A "mischievous curiosity," incurable insomnia, and a refusal to be housebroken made Elmer "rather toilsome to attend." These traits finally won him more permanent housing at the Woodland Park Zoo in Seattle — where perhaps even now Elmer, in true badgerlike fashion, is digging his way to freedom.

Black-Footed Ferret *(Mustela nigripes)*

It is "a robber baron securely established in the village of his helpless peasantry . . . . Its mating habits, call notes, love notes, song and amusements are wholly unknown. We know that it . . . lives like a mouse in a cheese, for the hapless Prairie-dogs are its favorite food." Thus did Ernest Thompson Seton describe in 1929 what is today North America's rarest and most endangered mammal, the black-footed ferret.

In keeping with its covert nature, *Mustela nigripes* hides behind a mask. The striking black band that runs across its large eyes helps to obscure the ferret's face when it pops its head out of a prairie dog burrow for a quick scan of the surroundings. The mask may also serve as a shield against the sun's glare on the open plains where the ferret is found. For additional camouflage, the ferret's buff-colored coat blends well with the dry, light-colored soil of the prairie; it turns lighter on the underparts and almost white on the forehead, throat, and muzzle. A dark, vertical stripe in the pubic area helps field observers distinguish the male from the female. Coordinating with its mask, the ferret's feet, legs, and last fourth of the tail are black. Its length is normally twenty-four inches; its weight, one and one-half pounds. Altogether, this animal presents a picture of elegance in color and design—that is, to the few who have been fortunate enough to see one.

Mammalogist Victor Cahalane, in a search throughout North America to determine its status, recorded only sixty-four of these animals for the period 1948-52. Out of this number, forty-two sightings were considered reliable. Records from individual states read like missing person reports: Nebraska, 1916-49—twelve specimens; Montana, 1948-52—seven; Colorado, 1948-52—four; Kansas, 1957-74 — one. The reports are often inaccurate. Long-tailed weasels are frequently mistaken for ferrets because of their size and the face mask worn by some subspecies. (The biggest mistake occurred in Montana, where one reported "ferret" turned out to be a cougar.) Even in South Dakota, where the ferret is relatively more numerous, the researcher who sights its slim silhouette through binoculars considers himself lucky indeed. The researcher has several strikes against him: the ferret is nocturnal in habits, quick in movement, and scarce in number. Hopeful observers have waited at a prairie dog town for days; most leave, however, without ever seeing this mysterious mustelid.

The black-footed ferret was not even acknowledged until Audubon and Bachman in 1851 first described a specimen stuffed with sagebrush which had been sent to them from Fort Laramie, Wyoming. Typical of its elusive nature, the original specimen was mislaid; it was twenty-five years before another ferret was reported.

The Indians of the Plains had lived in long association with the ferret and held it in special regard. The Sioux called it the "black-faced prairie dog" and believed that he who killed a ferret would either have bad luck or become hypnotized. (The Indian's sign for the ferret is a "Z", represented by an arm held up with the elbow and wrist crooked into a Z formation. He makes this motion, and at the same time points at something black and passes his hand across his face. In Montana, Blackfoot and Cheyenne chiefs decorated their headdresses with ferret pelts. Others, like the Crow, used the skins in ceremonies. The Pawnees of Nebraska called the ferret "ground dog." They believed that if the ferret sat up and looked at someone while working its jaws in a chewing motion, that person would immediately be cut to pieces and die.

The black-footed ferret's closest relative is the Old World ferret, known as the Siberian polecat (*Mustela eversmanni*), whose forebears probably migrated to North America via the Bering Land Bridge in prehistoric times.

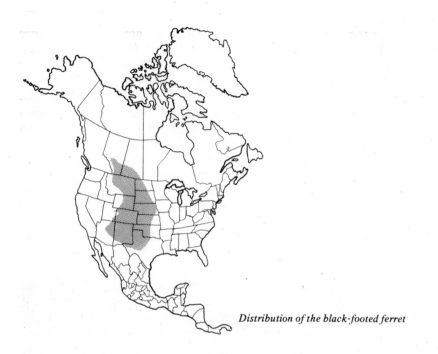

Distribution of the black-footed ferret

On this continent, the original range for the black-footed ferret is associated with the short-grass prairies east of the Rockies — the wide-open spaces that extend from southern Alberta and Saskatchewan south to Arizona, New Mexico, and Texas. More succinctly, the ferret's range nearly coincides with that of the black-tailed prairie dog, its chief and favorite food.

Seton, when he wrote about the black-footed ferret, had a premonition of things to come — things that did not augur well for the masked mustelid. In 1929, he wrote: "Now that the big Demon of Commerce has declared war on the Prairie-dog, that merry little simpleton of the Plains must go . . . and with the passing of the Prairie-dog, the Ferret, too, will pass." Thus far, his prediction has been amazingly accurate.

The "robber baron" and the "little simpleton" are ecologically bound together as predator and prey. The ferret depends upon the prairie dog, not only for food but for shelter. It lives in the "towns" built by the prairie dog, communities that vary from several to hundreds of burrows, each entrance surrounded by carefully constructed mounds of earth. Here, during the day, the plump prairie dogs come out of their burrows to feast on forbs or tender shoots of grass. Highly social, they often interrupt their feeding to greet each other with a chirp, a bark, or a kiss. By eating the grasses, prairie dogs keep the vegetation low for better vantage should a ferret come to town. When a ferret does appear, the first dog to see it sends out a warning, bobs up and

"A robber baron" of the Plains — the black-footed ferret.

down excitedly, and then does a fast disappearing act underground. Other sentinels in the danger area follow suit as the predator stalks through the town.

At sunset, the prairie dogs retire to their burrows. Sometimes they plug up the burrow entrance, like locking the door at night. Then it is the ferret's turn. Under cover of darkness, it steals about, disappearing down one hole after another in search of its sleeping prey. It kills and eats the prairie dog underground. The traces left are scant — only a few bones remain as evidence.

No one has yet seen a ferret kill a prairie dog in the wild. Conrad Hillman, a biologist who has spent many years studying the ferret in South Dakota, did see one ferret capture an adult prairie dog on the surface and drag it, kicking, down a burrow. The ferret reappeared some twenty minutes later with blood on its muzzle. In captivity, the ferret has been observed to attack the prairie dog from behind, biting into the neck and shoulder. In field experiments, tethered prairie dogs were placed near the burrow entrances. The ferrets were seen to approach them cautiously, grab them on the side of the neck, and drag them down the burrow. Interestingly, if the prairie dogs were so securely staked that the ferrets could not pull them down into the burrow, they would not eat the animal until the observer had left.

When leaving a burrow, the ferret backs out, passing the dirt from its front to its back feet and kicking it out behind. This operation creates a trench from one to ten feet long at the burrow entrance, one of the few telltale signs that a ferret is actually present in the dog town.

The prairie dog does not take this predation lying down, however. Often during the day it retaliates by plugging up ferret-occupied burrows. (These covered burrows are another sign to researchers of the possible presence of ferrets.) To confine the ferret, the prairie dog kicks dirt into the opening and then tamps it down with its nose or forehead. The effort is in vain, however, for the ferret seems to have no trouble escaping its plugged prison.

The prairie dog can also be openly aggressive towards its enemy, as seen from the field notes of biologist Richard Adrian: "Two ferrets are sighted with their heads out of the burrow. The prairie dogs have seen them and are moving toward the ferrets' burrow. The ferrets do not attack, even though the prairie dogs continue to move in on them. The lead prairie dog is advancing slowly, its head held high and its tail bushed out. One of the ferrets has its

A prairie dog, the ferret's favorite feast, scans its world for the enemy.

head and front legs over the mound surrounding the burrow . . . . The lead prairie dog is extremely cautious as it proceeds toward the ferret. It frequently jumps backward two or three steps, but then advances slowly. Now the prairie dog nips at one ferret; the ferret withdraws. Now one ferret advances and the prairie dog withdraws. This ferret moves slowly out of the burrow and is angling away from the prairie dog. The prairie dog rushes at the ferret, hits it and continues on. The ferret rolls over and back onto its feet. It returns to the burrow, and both ferrets descend. The prairie dog goes to the burrow and begins covering it."

The prairie dogs' consumption of food grasses is a menace to the cattleman. Thus, a relentless poisoning campaign has been waged against them and other "pests" since the 1930s. Strychnine-coated pellets, zinc phosphide, burrow fumigants, and suffocating cartridges have all been used in the battle. Most lethal is Compound 1080, or sodium monofluoractate, which, because of its stability, does not break down in the victim's body. There are secondary effects with this "nonspecific" poison: the prairie dog is poisoned, as well as any predator, such as the ferret, that eats the contaminated victim. Over the years, the efforts of animal control authorities to eradicate the prairie dogs have been so successful that they have been eliminated from much of their former range. This control, of course, does not help the black-footed ferret. The issue has been further clouded by the ironic role played by the Department of the Interior. Congressional directives charge the department with conflicting responsibilities: to administer rodent and pest control programs, and at the same time, to protect endangered wildlife. In the case of the ferret and the prairie dog, the two directives do not mix.

One of the principal objections during the 1960s to the government's conflicting policy was its method of making poisoning "safe" for the ferret. Field men were assigned to a dog town to determine whether ferrets were or were not present before a decision was made to set out poison. This was a virtually impossible task in light of the ferret's nocturnal and secret habits. Arguments among the U.S. Fish and Wildlife Service, the Bureau of Indian Affairs, ranchowners, and conservationists grew heated over whether it would be better to poison the prairie dogs first and do research on the ferret later, or to do research first and hold off on the poisoning. Meanwhile, no doubt ferret populations were affected by the continuing elimination of prairie dogs. As illustrated in South Dakota, the U.S. Bureau of Biological Survey has estimated that between 1923 and 1967 there was a 97 percent reduction in prairie dog habitat in a state which apparently shelters more ferrets than any other.

Two factors finally helped curtail some of the poisoning. First, the Endangered Species Act passed in 1966 was a victory for the ferret. *Mustela nigripes* was among the first fourteen mammals listed by the Secretary of the Interior. Second, an Executive Order issued in 1972 banned the use of poisons with secondary effects on federal lands or for federal programs. However, registered toxicants not believed to have secondary effects, such as strychnine or zinc phosphide, can still be used by the federal government, the state, and the private landowner. The situation gets stickier, for it seems that strychnine *can* be secondarily fatal to an animal like the ferret if the predator eats the intestinal tract of its poisoned prey. (Zinc phosphide is said to have no secondary effect.) In addition, there is a lot of poisonable federal land in South Dakota — national parks and grasslands, Forest Service land, a vast military range, and Indian reservations. Some of these areas are now under control programs.

Before poison is to be set out on any of these lands, a "presurvey" is required to determine whether or not ferrets are present. If either the ferret or its characteristic trenches are seen, that dog town is supposedly passed over. The Pine Ridge Indian Reservation is in the first stages of such a control program, one which will poison at least 50,000 acres of dog towns.

Once the ferret became an "endangered species," funds were appropriated to establish a breeding stock of captive animals at the U.S. Fish and Wildlife Research Center in Patuxent, Maryland. Here, Dr. Ray Erickson, assistant director for endangered wildlife research, supervises the study of five captive ferrets — three males and two females — in the hope that future generations of ferrets may be released into parks, refuges, and protected dog towns. Although the Research Center has had success with the ferret's close kin, the European ferret, so far the black-footed species has been uncooperative.

In the wild, field studies conducted since 1962 have resulted in new data about the ferret's life cycle. From examination of pregnant female ferrets found dead on the highways, it is believed that mating probably occurs in April, with birth in June. (Delayed implantation in the ferret remains unsolved.) During the summer months, the young are always attended by their mother, and there is no evidence that the male ferret assists in rearing the young. The mother alone cares for them, and field reports show that her activities are so secret that, until the little ferrets appear above ground in July, little can be learned about their behavior. In fact, it is difficult to tell which burrow contains them.

According to a report issued by the South Dakota Department of Game, Fish and Parks, in 1974, the following drama unfolded each night as darkness shielded the ferret family's movements: "Upon digging her way out of her burrow if it had been covered by industrious prairie dogs during the day, the mother ferret would look around with only her head showing . . . .

Long and low, the black-footed ferret waits to attack.

At times she appeared to be sniffing the air. After several minutes she would emerge and cautiously canvass burrows in the immediate area. If she became alarmed, she would run with a rapid bounding gait to the nearest burrow. Often her head would reappear so quickly that it seemed a second animal was present. At times she would stand up on her hind legs, presumably to get a better view or scent. After her safety standard was satisfied, she would proceed to and dig open, if necessary, the burrow containing the young.

"Finally the young would appear at the opening, first showing only their heads and gradually the foreparts of their bodies. Slowly, one by one, they would emerge from the burrow. If they were reluctant to leave the burrow, as they sometimes were, the mother would seize them individually by the nape and pull each one out. Frequently the mother would have to repeat this procedure several times before a young would remain outside. This shy behavior faded as the offspring grew in age and confidence. Then the mother was able to call the young out by uttering a repeated, low, plaintive 'ungh' note."

Following their mother's lead, the ferrets learned to move in single file with graceful bounds, like a miniature train. From June to mid-July the

The black-footed ferret claims its prey.

family stayed in the same general area of the dog town, but after this they began to extend their activities, probably because of the increasing food needs of the young. Observers also noted that by mid-July the young ferrets, then nearly half size, apparently were being weaned. "When one of the young, having been coaxed out of the burrow by its mother, attempted to nurse, she pushed it away. At the time, the mother was noticeably thin and unkempt from the demands of feeding and caring for the young. Her appearance contrasted with the fresh, sleek look of her offspring."

The mother was also seen dragging a dead adult prairie dog from one burrow to another for the young. Although this occurred several times, it was more convenient on other occasions to lead the little ferrets to an underground dinner than to drag the food home at night.

Around mid-July, the observers noted scuffling noises just below the burrow entrances, where the young were apparently having underground tussling matches. Dick Adrian, one of the authors of the South Dakota report, saw one playful ferret leap up and execute a midair somersault. On another occasion, he saw several walking on tiptoe, arching their backs and dancing about.

Additional ferret information has accumulated: they remain active during winter in temperatures down to -18 degrees; like mink and otter, they travel under and sometimes slide on top of snow; they have an odor closely resembling that of a mink; their diet is 90 percent prairie dog, although a few in captivity have eaten ground squirrels, mice, and other animals. As for probable predators, badgers, domestic dogs and cats, owls, and hawks are contenders. The automobile also takes its toll. Man's deliberate destruction of the prairie dog is, of course, the ferret's biggest threat. Toward man himself, interestingly enough, those ferrets observed in the wild show an amazing lack of fear and could often be approached within a few feet.

Conrad Hillman, the ferret field biologist for the Patuxent Wildlife Research Program, has spent endless nights searching with his spotlight for the ferret's green eyeshine. Through the efforts of Hillman, other wildlife biologists, conservationists, and even ranchers who are tolerant of the ferret-prairie dog program, certain areas are deliberately being left undisturbed for these animals. In 1973, U.S. Fish and Wildlife leased 467 acres of prairie dog towns where ferrets are known to exist. In addition, an agreement among the Department of Defense, the Department of the Interior, and the state of South Dakota has been initiated to ban all poisoning on the 42,240-acre Badlands Gunnery Range. Defenders of Wildlife has also contracted with the Rosebud Sioux Indians to protect the ferret and prairie dog on their 2 million-acre reservation. The agreement prohibits plowing the land and killing either animal.

In September 1973, a Black-footed Ferret and Prairie Dog Workshop was held in Rapid City, South Dakota. Over 100 delegates from a fourteen-state area met to discuss the ferret-prairie dog problem: ranchers; Indian landowners and leaseholders; biologists; state and federal personnel; and representatives from the National Wildlife Federation, Audubon Society, and Defenders of Wildlife.

From this swap of facts and information, it became obvious that much information is still lacking about ferret behavior. However, researchers have learned many of the ferret's secrets; they can now recognize signs of its presence and know that fall is the best season for spotting it. Hillman also reported that the occasional discovery of road kills and the dispersal of young ferrets in fall further suggest that the ferret's movements may be more extensive than originally thought.

Although the participants disagreed about how the problem should be managed, all acknowledged that management was necessary. It is obvious by now that prairie dog populations have been reduced drastically. As for ferret sightings: Nebraska — 13 since 1965; New Mexico — 3 since 1969; North Dakota — 10 since 1966; Oklahoma — 51 since 1961 (many questionable); Montana — none for 20 years; Colorado — 6; Kansas — extirpated. Only South Dakota with over 200 sightings since 1960 has any number, most of these reports occurring in Mellette County in the western part of the state.

Why save the black-footed ferret? E. M. Merrick, a delegate from the National Wildlife Federation, had what he admitted was a fanciful but nevertheless reasonable response: the ferret represents an irreplaceable gene pool which may benefit mankind. In spite of the abundance of prairie dogs in its environment, the ferret does not eat itself out of house and home. Merrick suggested that "an understanding of the biological mechanism involved in the ferret's 'natural birth control' or auto-systemic fertility control may provide a necessary and valuable contribution to man in solving one of his most pressing problems."

The ferret's future is questionable, its fate as yet undetermined. Management of both ferret and prairie dog remains the only realistic key to their conservation. As one wildlife biologist put it: "If we mismanage the ferret, probably only the ferret will suffer. But if we mismanage the prairie dog, both species will suffer. In either case, the black-footed ferret would probably become extinct." And in that case, Seton's prediction would come true, and it will be the end of the little robber baron of the Plains.

Striped Skunk *(Mephitis mephitis)*

Hooded Skunk *(Mephitis macroura)*

No one ever mistakes a skunk. No matter which kind it is — striped, spotted, hooded, or hognosed — one look at that plumed tail and those black and white markings leaves no doubt about its identity. Unlike most mammals, which are camouflaged in subtle browns and grays, the skunk is boldly attired in black and white — a coloration considered the greatest contrast visible to any of the normally colorblind mammals. It is thus quickly identified by both man and beast.

There appears to be good enough reason for this marked coloration, for the skunk does not need to hide. It has instead a subtle form of defense, as effective as any in nature: two glands on either side of the anal tract containing an odious sulphuric compound called N-butyl mercaptan. Fired by the contraction of the skunk's powerful hip muscles, this acrid, yellowish liquid can shoot up to twelve feet with awful accuracy. The results are demoralizing, as everyone who has ever aroused a skunk can verify. Two or three drops of this vile solution can be smelled for more than half a mile in all directions. Furthermore, a mature skunk's arsenal is loaded with four to six successive discharges, should the occasion warrant. So the best advice to anyone about to be hit by this four-legged fumigator is — make tracks!

The skunk's spray is so obnoxious that it causes painful burning of the eyes and may even bring on nausea and weakness. Getting rid of the stench is another problem. Many methods have been tried. For the skin, a couple of washings with gasoline may help; or alternating baths in ammonia and, of all things, tomato juice, followed by a good scrubbing with strong soap (outdoors, of course). For the clothing, trappers try a smoking technique over burned juniper or cedar leaves. Other suggestions are chemically oriented: soaking the clothes in gasoline, ammonia, chloride of lime, or a diluted solution of sodium hypochlorite. Washing the skunked clothing only delays the consequences, however, for on rainy days the smell mysteriously returns. Probably the most effective answer is to sacrifice the items to a roaring fire.

On the skunk's behalf, it must be said that not everyone finds its stench revolting. Naturalist John Burroughs described it as "tonic and bracing." Others, like mammalogist Victor Cahalane, find a "little" skunk scent rather pleasant. In fact, skunk musk *can* be put to good use as a fixative for perfume, and its oil was once popularly used as a treatment for rheumatism.

Thus, with supreme self-confidence, the sturdy little skunk meanders about unmolested. It does not hurry; it does not need to. It can be found almost anywhere from city park to wilderness area and is the most common member of the weasel family by a large, odoriferous margin.

Skunks eat almost anything that jumps or flits through their small realm. Their teeth are designed for a varied diet; they retain the long canines and the sharp incisors of their more carnivorous relatives, but have fairly flat molars for chewing fruits and vegetation. Small rodents, reptiles, and amphibians are also on the menu. "It is fond of the juicy larvae of bumblebees and yellow jackets," writes one Idaho naturalist, "and it will almost demolish a colony in one visit. Upon approaching an apiary cautiously and scratching on the hive to invite the bees outside, it will, indifferent to fury and stings, eat as many as it can pick out of its fur . . . . " Whether stalking grubs or grasshoppers or catching crickets, cutworms, or caterpillars, the skunk is one of the most important insect predators among mammals. In addition, thanks to its generalized habits, it can live in areas that will not support larger carnivores or those with specialized food habits.

There are four kinds of skunks in North America: striped, spotted, hooded, and hognosed. Collectively, they are called polecats or woodpussies; the French Canadians called them *mouffettes* or *enfants du diable.*

The striped skunk is about the size of a cat, marked with a bold white head patch, which divides into a V stripe, extending from stem to stern of its otherwise shiny black body. Males of this species weigh between four and ten pounds and are from two to two and one-half feet long, including an eight- to ten-inch bushy tail. Females are slightly smaller.

More common than its spotted relative, the striped skunk is at home throughout the United States, except for the southern tip of Florida. It seems to prefer open fields, bottom lands, and meadows to densely timbered areas, so much so that the vast cleared logging and agricultural lands across country have enhanced its home range. The striped skunk is absent from Alaska and the northern latitudes of Canada. This absence in colder climes occurs because striped skunks, particularly females and their young, become semidormant as the winter days approach. (In the Far North, this dormant period would probably last longer than the skunks could tolerate without food.) Elsewhere, the skunks usually put on fat in the fall and den up in a borrowed raccoon or rabbit burrow, often grouping in a shallow hibernation. Such skunk snugglings are often comprised of several females and one possessive male who stays with his harem until the weather warms. In the more southerly parts of their range, there is less winter sleeping, or none at all, and some skunks remain active throughout the year.

Mephitis mephitis is the striped skunk's scientific name — an appropriate Latin word meaning a double dose of a "noxious or pestilential exhalation from the ground." When alarmed, *Mephitis* resorts to its famous defense: first it stamps its front feet in a stiff-legged warning, then turns its back on the object of its wrath, raises its tail, and fires. Whew! The little sharpshooter is accurate. Only the great horned owl will dare prey on the striped skunk regularly, and many of these birds reek of skunk musk when they themselves are caught. Although coyote, cougar, or mink faced with starvation may prey upon the skunk as a last resort, these incidents are rare.

As a result of their effective defense system, skunks have developed a false sense of security. Unable to differentiate between hayfield and highway, they expect everything to come to a halt when they step out on the road. At such times, they encounter their most deadly predator, *Automobilius americanus*. Many "skunk hollows" — as well as skunked autos — bear the unforgettable odor of mashed mephitines.

Though almost free from enemies, skunks are not free from disease. They are subject to rabies and worm-caused sinus infections which can be fatal. Parasites, external and internal, also take their toll: lice, fleas, ticks, and mites may attack from the outside, while roundworms and flatworms go to work internally. Domesticated skunks are also subject to pneumonia.

Striped skunks are born in a litter of four to seven (usually five) between

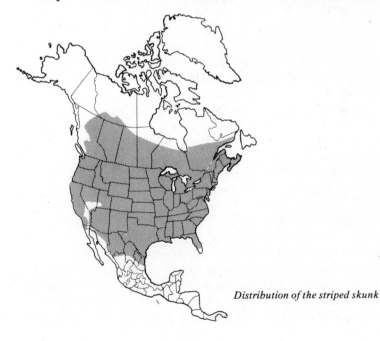

Distribution of the striped skunk

95

*The striped skunk is marked with a bold white head patch,
which divides into a V stripe extending from stem to stern.*

April and mid-May after nine weeks' gestation. Though they are blind,
helpless, and nearly fuzzless at birth, their white stripes are immediately
visible. After three or four weeks, they may try to leave the birthing burrow
for sunlight but are promptly hauled back by their mother. She continues to
bring them food — mice, snakes, crayfish, beetles, grasshoppers — until at
six weeks she leads them forth in a small black and white band.

Few sights are as charming as that of a mother skunk on an evening's
foray with her string of babies wobbling behind her. In their training, they
troop to the marshes for frogs and learn to smell out turtle eggs and dig them
up with their tiny but tough front claws. They learn to locate insect larvae

and beetles and birds' nests hidden in the rushes. At nine weeks, each member of the brood wears a plumed tail and a thick, glossy coat. They are mature by autumn, equipped with a well-developed stench-making apparatus and a capacity to use it. They breed in their first year, one male mating with more than one female.

Skunks make good pets when descented. They are said to be intelligent, peppy, and affectionate, particularly the females. Best trained when young, they can grow up on a diet of cat food, with a little fruit for variety.

Because of its stench that stays and its occasional raids on henhouses, the striped skunk has earned a foul reputation. Some patience, a few fence posts,

The hooded skunk's tail is as long as its body and its nape hair spreads into a cape or hood.

Distribution of the hooded skunk

perhaps a sprinkling of moth balls or naphthalene flakes if the skunk is living under the house — and above all the knowledge that these animals are fine insect fighters and mousers — should be considered before condemning them.

The southern cousin within the genus *Mephitis* is the hooded skunk, *Mephitis macroura*. Generally, this skunk looks like its striped relative, except for its large tail, which is as long as its body, and its nape hair which spreads into a cape or hood. It may wear one of two basic color patterns: either the whole back, including the tail, will be white, or the back will be almost all black, with two widely separated white stripes along the sides.

In the valley country of southern New Mexico and Arizona, in the Big Bend region of south Texas and further south to Nicaragua, the hooded skunk lives along stream edges, canyons, or brush bottoms, resting during the hot days and foraging for skunk fare at night.

Spotted Skunk *(Spilogale gracilis, Spilogale putorius)*

The spotted skunk is the peppy, high-strung member of the skunk group. Measuring between twelve and twenty-two inches long, it weighs three pounds at the most — the smallest of the four North American skunks. Thus, its generic name from the Greek is *Spilogale,* small striped carnivore.

Two species comprise the genus *Spilogale* to further describe this skunk: *gracilis,* the western variety, for its dainty appearance, and *putorius,* the eastern form, a name that speaks for itself.

Spilogale has a variety of nicknames, some of them misleading. Trappers know it as the "civet cat," although it is not a cat, nor is it related to the

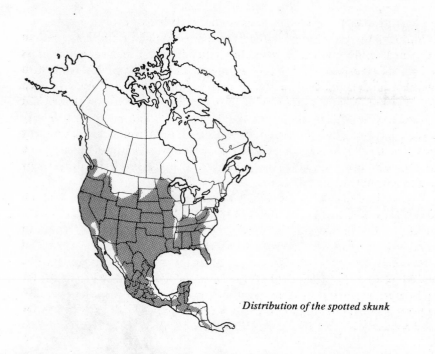

Distribution of the spotted skunk

European civets. It is also known as "phoby cat" or "hydrophobia skunk" because it is reputed to carry rabies. Unfortunately, this is a proper alias: skunks, both striped and spotted, have been known to attack unpredictably when infected with rabies, although reports of such contacts are extremely rare. False stories of hydrophobia sometimes occur because at mating season *Spilogale*'s behavior may get a little out of control. Under the influence of mating madness, it is known to attack other animals without cause. One love-crazed skunk reportedly invaded the sanctuary of a wolf's nursery. For no apparent reason, it picked up the wolf pups and shook the frightened babies by the ears.

Instead of sporting the bold stripes of *Mephitis mephitis*, the spotted skunk is splotched with white on its forehead and cheeks. The erratic white markings on its back and sides are actually broken white stripes. A white tail tip contrasts sharply with the jet background of its body.

Although their habits are similar, the spotted skunk is less common than the striped variety. Its range is smaller, extending sort of diagonally across the United States from Florida to Washington and on to southwestern British Columbia in Canada. For habitat, it prefers brushy and dry areas to open fields where it lives on a diet similar to that of its striped cousin. Because it requires less food than the larger skunk species, it can survive in the dry canyons and rimrocks of Nevada, New Mexico, or Arizona. Just about any place is home — a hollow, burrow, nook, or cranny, sometimes the attic of a house, or even the mummified carcass of a cow. In its den, it usually rests by day and goes out to hunt at night.

The spotted skunk is more high-strung and active than other skunk species. It forages about at all times of the year. Though all skunks swim, the spotted variety does so more readily. It is a capable climber and can sometimes be seen scrambling along fences or on the high rafters of outbuildings. It is quick to climb a tree in search of birds' nests or fruit, the only skunk to do so. Confident and fearless, it raids garbage cans and, for that matter, may decide to move right into or under the house. *Spilogale* also has a strange egg-breaking habit. For some unknown reason, it will throw eggs backwards through its legs, giving each egg a quick kick with its hind foot.

Dainty and playful, the spotted skunk is also prettier than the others. It has large, appealing eyes and an intelligent nature. But don't be misled by its beauty. In the wild, this nervous little high stepper has a short temper. Mammalogist Walter Dalquest has described its behavior as follows: "Whereas the striped skunk almost never throws its scent when trapped, the civet cat almost invariably does so, apparently when the trap closes about its legs. Striped skunks in traps move slowly and steadily but civet cats jump, roll, and squirm erratically."

One night while sleeping in an old building along the Tolt River in Washington, Dalquest was awakened by a stamping noise from the next room. "Investigation revealed a civet cat indulging in a series of short, stiff-legged hops. The forefeet were held slightly ahead and six or eight hops made. The animal would then relax, turn and prance off in a new direction." He wrote that the animal seemed to like the noise it made, and that the prancing may have been a form of play.

When threatened, the spotted skunk does a handstand and takes aim.

Prancing is also part of the skunk's defense display. The spotted skunk, rather than merely raising its tail in the air, puts more flair and flourish into its act. When threatened, it will do a handstand, throwing its whole body and hind legs into the air and bristling its tail. The full extent of its spotted back is thus exposed to an aggressor, a posture which it can maintain for five or six seconds at a time. If the predator does not move away immediately, a salvo of N-butyl mercaptan will be delivered posthaste.

The two spotted skunk species have different mating habits. The eastern variety mates in April and has a 50- to 65-day gestation before the young are born. Western spotted skunks mate in September, followed by a 180- to 200-day period of delayed implantation. Its young are born in May after a gestation period of 210 to 230 days. Litter size varies from two to six, and each little skunk weighs about one-third of an ounce. Over the first seven weeks of life, its eyes open and its teeth develop. By the eighth week, it is weaned, reaching full size in a little over three months. As an adult, it will encounter few predators except for the great horned owl — and the great horned automobile. Owl predation, however, is not as extensive in the spotted skunk as with other skunks, according to one man who studied owls for many years. Lewis Walker, in his *Book of Owls,* explains that the spotted skunk's trait of running on front feet when agitated, with tail end elevated, creates an anti-aircraft device against horned owls that blinds them at the moment of attack.

As for skunk fur, only the striped and spotted skunks are of any value. Deep and shiny, entire coats have been made of the pelts; however, most skins are used as trim on coats. The pelts are inexpensive, with more black coloring bringing a higher price. Only 867 skunks were trapped throughout Canada in 1973-74, bringing an average price of $1.48 per pelt. Hudson's Bay Company in New York, however, reports up to $4.00 per pelt. Though pelt prices are comparatively low, damage incurred by the trapper and his trappings can be high. The inconvenience of smoked clothing, tomato juice baths, or ammonia soakings does not give high priority to skunk trapping.

Not too many years ago, skunk fur was disguised under the pseudonym "black marten" or "Alaskan sable." Those who did not know what they had bought found out soon enough. On the first damp night, the little skunk — never one to go unnoticed — showed its true colors, sending out its own mysterious and distinctive smell.

Hognosed Skunk

(Conepatus mesoleucus, Conepatus leuconotus)

The hognosed skunk, distinguished by its long, bare, flexible snout, is easily identified but not often seen. Much like a hog, it roots around in search of an exclusive insect menu of beetles, crickets, or grasshoppers. It is aided in this search by long, heavy claws for overturning the soil. These claws and a pair of heavy shoulders have earned it the nickname "badger skunk."

Although little is known about the hognose, its habits seem to be similar to those of the striped skunk. It is equal in size to or larger than the striped variety, colored white above (including the whole tail) and black below.

The hognose is apparently a northern migrant from Mexico, where the species is more plentiful. Some authorities list two separate species for the hognose; however, these may be only geographical races of the same species. In the United States, it inhabits the desert valleys of southeast Arizona, southern Colorado, and southwest Texas. Probably a litter of one to four young is born each year after a gestation of about forty-two days.

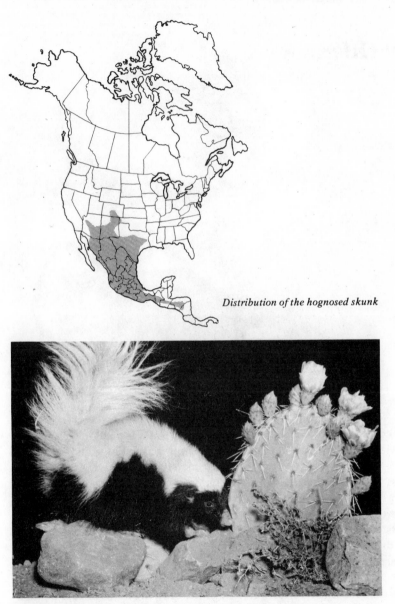

Distribution of the hognosed skunk

The hognosed skunk has a long, bare, flexible snout.

River Otter *(Lutra canadensis)*

"Alacris ad ludos est." Albertus Magnus, in the thirteenth century, thus described the otter: "It is quick to play." And play it does, its whole life through.

Those who have watched *Lutra canadensis*, the North American otter, tumbling and tobogganing down snow-covered hillsides or sliding down muddy riverbanks, have been treated to a magical moment in the animal world. Its playfulness has no apparent purpose — except for the sheer joy of sport and frolic. Gregarious and curious, the otter is the Good Time Charlie of the weasel family.

Perhaps because it is so well adapted and because food is plentiful, the otter has time for leisure. Most versatile of the mustelids, it is at ease on land and in fresh or salt water. Its legs are short and strong for land travel, yet easily tucked to its sleek sides when swimming after fish or poking about on river bottoms. Its broad head is designed with the eyes set high for peering above water while cruising almost totally submerged. Underwater, it is aided by a fine flare of stiff whiskers that act as feelers when it roots in the mud for frogs and minnows. When diving, the otter's ears and nose close tightly and its strong lungs hold enough oxygen for four minutes submerged. The strong, tapered tail serves as a rudder as it moves deftly through the water, and five webbed toes provide a broader surface for swimming and thrust. The action of its tail and toes, when combined with the fishlike undulations of its body, produces rapid twists and turns in the water. At the same time, tail and feet are never so cumbersome that the otter cannot travel many miles overland when it chooses.

Much of the otter's time is spent on land, where it runs along in a rippling motion — much the same way as an inchworm creeps along a branch, but many times faster. It can cover a territory of up to twenty-five miles within a week.

All in all, the otter's appearance is streamlined and tubular — ten to thirty-five pounds of muscular mustelid, measuring three to five feet in length, the third largest of the weasel tribe. Its dense fur is dark brown, shading to silvery gray-brown on the muzzle, throat, and underparts.

The river otter, alias the common otter, land otter, or Canada otter, is not strictly limited in habitat as long as water is nearby. All of North America, from placid lake to turbulent stream, is its playground. Along shrub-fringed waterways, beaver ponds, and other lowland watercourses, it may be found, as well as in the streams of the foothills and mountains.

Its home range may be fifteen miles or more, which the sociable otters will cover in small groups — perhaps up a river, branching off to a lake, then to headwaters of a tributary, across land to a brook and back to the river again — all in a couple of weeks. Nor does it adhere to a rigid diet; fish, crayfish, rabbits, ducks, frogs, salamanders, muskrats, and aquatic insects are all consumed.

The otter eats less fish than is commonly expected. In fact, captive otters fed fish exclusively have become ill. Food habit studies in Oregon show that otters do depend on salmon for their winter diet and that the low density of otters does not deplete these fish. A six-year study in the Great Lakes region showed that nongame fish were the main prey species in this region, along

Distribution of the river otter

with frogs and crayfish — a particular otter favorite. By taking nongame fish that might prey on species like trout, the otters are actually a boon to the fisherman.

Availability of food rather than altitude determines the otter's distribution. Thus, it is found on the highest lakes if fish are present. In the Pacific Northwest, it is widely distributed near both fresh and salt waters, where it hunts at all seasons and hours. In British Columbia, these animals are associated with ocean shorelines and larger waterways throughout the province. They are less often seen in inland areas. The seacoast, lakes, and waterways of Washington and Oregon also provide suitable habitat. Some river otters have taken up residence around the San Juan Islands of Puget Sound where the local inhabitants consider them a valuable asset.

Consequently, otters play on residential floats and beaches. They peer out from under pontoons and live in boathouses along the shore. They have adapted almost completely to a marine environment, using freshwater streams for den sites and salt water for feeding on herring or rockfish. In Idaho, where Merriam observed in 1891 that otters were common, they are much less abundant today. Less than 100 are taken by Idaho trappers each year. In California, where it swims in the lakes and marshes of the northernmost area, the otter is completely protected by law.

Along stream or river banks, the otter makes a den under tree roots or rock ledges, in deserted beaver lodges, or in hollow logs. When leaving the water, it usually rolls about in the grass or snow to dry off, and it leaves ample evidence of its presence — a trail of tracks including dragging tail marks and occasional droppings laced with remains of crustaceans or fish. Otters also twist grass tufts together for use as scent stations near the mouths of dens or on small elevations. This habit appears to be as much territorial as sexual, for it occurs at all times of the year. Emil Liers, a long-time otter authority, observed that when several otters travel together each one tries to be the last to leave its scent at a "station."

With few enemies but man, and possibly certain parasitic worms, the otter is free to follow a life of fishing and fun. If alarmed or angered, however, it will emit its mustelid musk and resort to a vocabulary of calls: a snort or cough in alarm, a scream in anger, sometimes a friendly chirp. One common group sound is a low-keyed chuckling noise that seems to be associated with pleasant feelings while grooming, copulating, or communicating at close range. This sound may be imitated by closing the lips and saying "huh-huh-huh" as deeply as possible in rapid succession.

When together, otters help each other, a trait that trappers will take advantage of when trying to catch them. The trapper will place several snares together, hoping to add to his bag when the first otter caught calls for help. In his book *Otters*, C. J. Harris describes a similar situation in captivity that occurred the first time a pair of his otters went upstairs (which, he says, otters will always do if stairs are available). The male was at first incapable of getting down again. He called to the female at the bottom, who at once "climbed back to him, and then led him slowly down, step by step, talking to him all the way." Emil Liers, too, wrote about the otter's loyalty: "If another otter is in trouble," he says, "or even a human they are attached to, they will pitch in to fight off danger." He describes one occasion when a strange dog bit him on the hand, tearing one finger to the bone. His otters loose in the yard came to the rescue and drove the dog from the premises.

Otters make delightful pets — for the patient owner. They are bright, friendly, and very much "contact" animals. At the same time, they are expensive to keep, willful, inquisitive (i.e., destructive), strong, and often short-tempered.

The otter's thick fur makes a long-lasting pelt. In fact, it is rated by furriers as more durable than any other. In Canada, about 18,000 pelts were auctioned in 1973 at an average price of $41, with particularly fine specimens going for $60. Alaska harvests between 1,000 and 4,000 every year; Washington averages 800 and Oregon 300. Prices range from $25 to $65 per pelt. The highest prices are paid for prime pelts from Alaska and northern Canada. Unlike other furs, ottter fur has been consistently high-priced over the years.

Perhaps the otter's most distinctive trait is intelligence. Curious creatures, they will fiddle with objects until they can pull them apart. Ancient records attest to their trainability: Chinese fishermen in the ninth century used otters to herd fish and drive them into waiting nets. Otters can learn to perform by watching and imitating. Liers reported that while hunting one day, his dog was unable to reach a shot duck. As a test, one of Liers' pet otters was turned loose into the dense foliage and successfully retrieved the fallen fowl. Thereafter, his otter became an excellent retriever.

Otters also have a good sense of direction. The British Columbia Provincial Museum cites a record of a semitame pair of otters that were transported from Victoria harbor on Vancouver Island to Vancouver's Stanley Park Zoo on the mainland. They escaped and three weeks later were back in their old haunts in Victoria. This little jaunt amounted to a lengthy trip across the Strait of Georgia, past many islands en route. The minimum distance involved was seventy miles, with a minimum water crossing of fifteen miles.

The otter's greatest passion is play. It will play alone, in groups, with other animals, or with people. It spends much time rolling in the grass, somersaulting underwater, frolicking in the snow, chasing its tail, or playing hide and seek. It will juggle a pebble in its paws or balance a stick on the end of its nose like a trained seal. Sometimes, on larger rivers, it will shoot the

River otters rest on a dock.

rapids, riding along with head erect on the watch for rocks and snags. Its most popular pastime is snow sliding or, in warmer seasons, mud sliding. Alone or in a happy little band it climbs a riverbank, tucks the forepaws close to its sides, and throws itself headfirst down the slide into the water. These slides may be twenty-five feet long, and there are many variations in the otter's tobogganing technique: sometimes the hind feet are used for pushing, sometimes a limb is held out for braking. The belly sliding can go on for hours, with each individual waiting its turn — just for the fun of it all.

In the water, the whole family spends time roughhousing — tossing pebbles or shells, grabbing one another and rolling over and over, splashing, teasing, and playing tag.

Springtime saddles the fun-loving otter with family responsibilities. Though breeding and delivery dates vary with latitude, breeding usually occurs in winter or spring and gestation extends from 288 to 380 days due to delayed implantation. Thus most litters are born in March or April in a borrowed burrow, perhaps a vacant beaver lodge, with entrances above or below the waterline. Males may mate with more than one female, but they generally spend most of their time with only one mate. Females may breed again shortly after giving birth.

An otter litter usually consists of two or three pups, although it may vary from one to four. The pups are blind and toothless and have fuzzy dark coats. They weigh about one-fourth of a pound. In seven weeks their eyes open, after which they remain in the den for nearly five weeks more. Then the pups are ready to come out and play on land with their mother. They are weaned in the fourth month. During all this time, the mother hides and shields the young from every possible intruder, including their father. When their waterproof fur coats thicken at about three months, swimming lessons begin, a time when the mother otter teaches the pups the skill they will eventually perform better than all but sea mammals.

Strange as it may seem for such an aquatic species, the little otters are often afraid of water. Many reports confirm that they have to be coaxed and forced into water over their heads. Liers observed that the mother otter sometimes had to drag a pup by the scruff of the neck or take it on her own back out into deep water. She would then submerge, leaving the pup to paddle its own canoe. Once over the initial fear, the little otters swim with skill. At this time, the father is permitted to join in the upbringing.

In training, the male otter often leads the way on family forays. Both parents teach the pups how to outswim and corner a fish in holes along stream banks. They are especially trained to root around in the mud for debris at the bottom of streams and ponds, where much of their food is found. In time, the pups learn to swim well under water, as well as to skim the surface with head partially exposed and to undulate like a dolphin. Overland hunting finds the mother in the lead followed by a string of pups. Liers has observed that if a pup gets too venturesome and tries to rush ahead, the mother nips it on the nose; the punished pup drops down and lies very still until she nudges it to move again.

As they become more competent swimmers and hunters, the family fun begins. There is much romping and playing in this gregarious group, although they remain together for only eight short months, after which the family disbands. The young otters then wander off, sometimes in pairs, seeking pools and rivers of their own for an active life of fishing and frolic.

Sea Otter *(Enhydra lutris)*

With its bewhiskered, quizzical face, bright eyes, button nose, and winning ways, the sea otter is the charmer of the weasel family. As a crowning glory, it wears the most exquisite and expensive fur coat of any mammal. It is no small wonder that this is a most prized and unique inhabitant of the Pacific coast.

Among its many distinctions, the sea otter *(Enhydra lutris)* is the largest of the mustelids and the only ocean-going member of the tribe. Males can weigh up to 100 pounds, females about 75 pounds, both stretching to five feet from sensitive nose to stout tail. Because of its marine adaptation, the otter is also classified as a sea mammal, but as a member of this group, which includes seals, dolphins, and whales, it is the smallest in size.

The sea otter is the most specialized of the weasel family. It is adapted to a small ecological area along the rocky coasts of Alaska and California, which is only a fraction of its original range. It formerly inhabited a coastal area from northern Japan around the North Pacific and south to Baja

114

California. Today, it lives in intertidal waters at depths up to twenty fathoms, where it dives for its food of sea urchins, abalone, mussels, or crab.

The otter is able to stay under water for five or six minutes, although its dives usually last little more than a minute. Once it has found food, the otter surfaces with its catch tucked under its arm in loose folds of skin. In its right paw it carries a rock. Lying blissfully on its back with its chest for a table, it uses the rock as a tool to break open the shell. Eyes closed in contentment, it devours its catch. It is usually the California sea otter that is spotted using a rock; rarely does the northern sea otter indulge in this pastime. Nevertheless, one of the Aleutian otters transplanted to the Tacoma Aquarium, when handed some clams and a rock, went right to work pounding them against his chest.

Wildlife biologist K. R. Hall and others believe the otter's use of a tool is a specific behavioral adaptation. It has "no special relevance to the evolution of the sort of intelligent, anticipatory skills which are most highly developed in man and which he uses for the manufacture of a standard set of tools to be kept in store and used on different occasions for various purposes." The otter's behavior is likened to that of gulls and ravens, who use gravity to break clam and mussel shells by dropping them on rocky surfaces.

This otter's true element is the sea. On land, when it hauls out to rest or preen its fur, it is heavy-bodied and slow. But at sea it is comfortable, usually floating on its back with the head and tail — or even a webbed foot — protruding from the kelp beds that are favored resting areas. Sometimes it sleeps wrapped in strands of kelp beyond the surf, where it rises and falls peacefully on the incoming sea. Bobbing up and down, it folds its front paws against its furry body and sometimes raises a paw to shield its eyes from the sun. Often its feet and tail extend out of the water for long periods, a practice that some scientists believe relates to thermoregulation or the acquisition of vitamins from the sun.

Along the rocky northwest coast, the sea otter drifts and dives in a sometimes hostile climate of cold winds and waves. To survive, it is equipped with strong, webbed hind feet and a horizontally flattened tail; these work together to produce deep dives and maneuverability. On the surface, alternating strokes of the hind flippers propel the otter along on its back, its preferred means of locomotion atop the waves. Its feet and tail function like a cetacean's flukes — the only non-cetacean to swim this way. Retractile claws,

Sea otters float on their backs at sea.

an adaptation not present in other mustelids, are aids for grasping shells and for passing food to its mouth. Its flattened molars are also adapted for crushing the shells of any food it brings up. The sea otter is the only mustelid with no functional anal scent glands.

Its fur is crucial for survival. Unlike other mammals that have returned to the sea, the otter lacks the insulating fat layer necessary for maintaining body warmth in the chilly Pacific waters. Instead, it has survived by means of its fur, which is extremely dense, interspersed sparingly with guard hairs. Each hair is about an inch long and elliptical in shape — fine at the root, thicker in the center, and very fine at the tip — thus allowing the outer fur to become wet but trapping a blanket of air next to the otter's skin to provide insulation and substantial buoyancy.

To maintain this buffer against the cold, the sea otter must clean itself constantly so that no dirt, oil, slime, or debris will interfere with the air layer. When the insulating mechanism fails through contact with oil, waste detergents, fish slime, or filth accumulated during long air or sea transplant voyages, the otter will die of shock or chill. Thus, the sea otter's almost obsessive grooming is an instinctive technique for suvival. Captive otters have been known to spend half of their daylight hours in this pastime. Fortunately, because it lives in a uniform climate, the otter does not undergo a dramatic fur molt that would leave it vulnerable; instead, throughout the year, at various places on the body, individual hairs are in molt while others are at rest.

The sea otter uses its paws and sometimes its foreclaws to groom and condition its fur. Turning and twisting its loose-skinned body, it rubs the fur with its paws to squeeze water out. A variety of techniques are used: sometimes it rolls in a ball in order to reach the lower back; sometimes it takes loose belly skin, stretches it over a foreleg, presses the water out, and licks it away with the tongue. Before falling asleep on the surface, the otter rolls over and over, smoothing and cleaning any food particles from the fur. For a final touch, it turns tummy down in the water, bends its head under, and blows air into the fur, all the while busily rubbing the sides and belly with its forepaws. This action provides aeration and a little extra "lift" for snoozing at the surface. If the otter is to rest on land, it will go through a ten-minute grooming routine before leaving the water and will continue drying off after it hauls out. Casual observers usually think the otter is scratching for ectoparasites, but this is false — the sea otter harbors none.

Much as its fur is a blessing to the sea otter, it has also been its undoing. The fur feels like long-napped velvet and looks like rich chocolate flecked with silvery gold. The substructure is an intense melding of smoky-gray underfur hairs (by far the most numerous), covered by guard hairs that vary widely in diameter and length. The result? The most exquisite combination of deep, dense, lustrous, soft, and durable animal hair in the world. For its fur, then, it is no surprise that man became the sea otter's chief enemy.

In 1741, Vitus Bering, a Danish explorer in the service of Russia, discovered the sea otter when his crew was shipwrecked on the Commander

Islands. A year later, the survivors of this ill-fated expedition returned to their home port of Kamchatka, bringing with them not only hundreds of sea otter pelts but the sure knowledge as well that there were thousands more for the taking. Word of the rich fur spread rapidly, and along with it the relatively swift demise of the sea otter. Naturally docile and trusting, the animals were easy targets for the fur traders, and a program of slaughter which was to last 170 years was well on its way. Much blood was shed in the process; many Aleuts and Russians lost their lives in the quest for fur. As northwest exploration and commerce increased, the major cause of it all — the sea otter — began to disappear. By 1867, the year of the Alaska purchase, Russia had exported Alaskan furs worth many times what she received for the Great Land itself. A large percentage of these were sea otter pelts.

The United States took up where Russia left off. More than 47,000 otters were killed between 1881 and 1890. Ten years later, only 127 otters could be found. Pelt prices during this period soared to a high of $1,125 for a single pelt. (In later years, they were to bring $2,000 to $3,000.) Finally, in 1911 an international treaty gave protection to what few otters remained. All in all, the 170 years of unregulated slaughter had claimed probably half a million sea otters.

Miraculously, between 1,000 and 2,000 sea otters did manage to survive. Slowly but surely, in the remote reaches of the Pacific, the species made a comeback. Though they now occupy only one-fifth of their original range, the protected otters continue to increase. The highest concentration occurs in the Aleutian Islands, some of which are now experiencing an otter boom of 5 percent a year.

Off the coast of California, another band of 100 otters also survived the exploitation of the 1800s. Gradually, these animals have reproduced until they now number well over 1,800. The rocky 140-mile coastline between Monterey and Point Conception has been a perfect habitat for them, enhanced by the presence of abalone, a favorite sea otter food. The otter's passion for abalone has more recently caused a major conflict with commercial fishermen who resent the increasing sea otter depredations on an already rare resource. Two groups, the "Friends of the Abalone" and the "Friends of the Sea Otter," have formed to dispute the problem, but biologists stress that the only answer to maintaining healthy populations of both species is the establishment of a regulated management program. More

A subadult sea otter lies on its back on an Amchitka beach in typical defensive posture. The claws on the front paws are shown in retracted position.

recently, the expanding otters have moved into the Pismo clam beds, much to the chagrin of sportsmen and professional diggers.

Enhydra lutris disappeared completely in Oregon, Washington, and British Columbia after the 1800s. Transplant efforts in recent years may help bring them back, but the results are still uncertain. These programs have been undertaken with the joint cooperation of game departments from

Oregon, Washington, Alaska, and British Columbia, and the U.S. Fish and Wildlife Service. There have been setbacks in the process from heavy expenditures involved and difficulties in transporting these delicate animals.

In 1970 and 1972, British Columbia received eighty-nine sea otters from Amchitka and Prince William Sound. Those that survived the trip were released along the northwest coast of Vancouver Island near Brooks Peninsula. There has been no definite trace of them since, but B.C. game officials emphasize that though this is prime otter habitat, it is not prime human habitat. The animals, hidden in hundreds of inaccessible coves or camouflaged in drifting kelp beds, are virtually impossible to spot. Some have been reported on the south end of the Queen Charlotte Islands and near Barkley Sound, but these areas are hundreds of miles from the transplant site.

Washington received fifty-nine sea otters in 1969 and 1970. These were released near Point Grenville on the Olympic Peninsula, a former sea otter habitat. Because of the traumas of transport and the difficulty of keeping their fur clean, at least fourteen died during or after the first effort. Mortality on the second try appears to have been less (two known dead); the otters were held for three days, during which they adjusted to the new surroundings and cleaned themselves thoroughly before entering the cold Pacific once again. Otter sightings have been sketchy since, most of them occurring in the La Push area, some forty miles north of the transplant site. A 1974 aerial survey listed eight sea otters at Destruction Island, and another otter closer to the mainland. Among the group, there was at least one pup.

Oregon's transplant efforts appear to be paying off too, although U.S. Fish and Wildlife biologists warn that there is absolutely no assurance yet of success. Ninety-three were released in 1970 and 1971; seven were lost from shock and another found dead a year later. Since then, the highest number of sea otters sighted amounts to twenty-three, and combining various observations, there is evidence that fifteen pups have been born. If this small population can survive natural problems, such as heavy winter storms, which can prevent them from diving for food; or unnatural problems, like the rifle bullets of hunters, the damage of oil slicks, or pollution, the otters have the basic ingredients they need for survival: secluded rocky coasts and a shallow ocean floor encrusted with a plentiful supply of sea urchins.

The present sea otter population, from Alaska to California, is believed to be well over 50,000 — a good comeback for a special species. The otter is faring so well that a limited number of pelts were harvested in 1962 and 1963. These skins were auctioned in January 1968; prices varied from $80 to $280 each, with one lot of four rich skins bringing $2,300 per pelt.

Few people enter the "real world" of the sea otter. Its habitat is remote, inhospitable, and inaccessible. One firsthand observer is wildlife biologist Karl Kenyon, who for over fifteen years tracked, tagged, and studied these elusive animals. His research conducted on Amchitka Island in the Aleutian chain brought to light many facts about the sea otter's lifestyle. He observed on Amchitka that they habitually segregate themselves by sex, tending to occupy distinct male and female areas throughout the year. After two years of age, initial breeding occurs. At mating season, which takes place anytime, but

Distribution of the sea otter

121

most often from late fall to winter, the male leaves his bachelor's quarters in quest of a mate. He swims about, sometimes rising high in the water to look for a female stretched out on the rocks. When he encounters a receptive partner, the two roll and splash in the water, nuzzling and fondling one another with their forepaws. In the process of mating, the male will sometimes bite the female's nose with his teeth. Copulation takes place in the

Sea otter mother with her pup.

water, after which the pair stays together for a few days before separating. Twelve or thirteen months later, a single fuzzy yellow sea otter pup is born.

Though no one has ever reported witnessing a sea otter birth, there is some evidence that it may occur either on land or at sea. The pup can be born in any month and weighs four or five pounds. It is helpless when it enters a rather cold and inhospitable world, entirely dependent on its mother, who is a model of solicitude. She leaves the pup's side only to dive for food, sometimes anchoring the little one with strands of kelp. Bobbing about on the surface like a small yellow cork, the pup may kick its hind legs clumsily and cry out a high-pitched "waah-waah" when it feels neglected. The rest of the time, for well over a year, the mother sea otter grooms, nurses, cleans, and cuddles her pup. She carries it wherever she goes, usually swimming on her back with the pup clasped to her chest. If danger looms, the mother will instinctively dive, taking the pup with her. Unfortunately, if the pup is very small when this happens, it may drown.

The ties between mother and pup are very strong. One of many examples of this bond was recorded in 1910 by H. J. Snow: "For two hours we chased this otter, pursuing her between the rocks. The pup had been killed during the first hour, but she was holding it as firmly as ever, until a shot, striking one of her paws, made her drop it; and in trying to regain it she was once more wounded. Again and again she made the attempt, all the time giving utterance to the most plaintive and sorrowful cries."

Returning to the ship, Snow wrote later that night: "We had traveled some distance, when all at once, right under our stern, we heard the most unearthly crying imaginable; . . . another cry alongside showed us the dark form of the otter we had been chasing. It was now following the boat, lamenting the loss of her offspring."

Kenyon, while tagging otters on Amchitka Island in 1962, recorded reciprocal concern of the pup for its mother: "A mother and her 15-pound male pup were captured as they slept side-by-side on the beach today . . . . They were caught in separate nets. The pup was tagged first and released. Instead of heading for the water he ran to his struggling mother, put his forepaws on her side and began tearing at the net with his teeth and tried to climb up on her side. He had to be dragged away while a tag was placed on the mother's flipper. As soon as she was released, he rushed to her side and then followed her to the water. After a dive of about 50 meters, the two came up. The pup immediately clasped his mother about the neck and she pulled him towards her with her forepaws."

Swimming sessions begin while the pup is practically helpless. First, it learns to paddle belly down, then graduates to its lifelong favored position for swimming, on its back. It also begins to dive. At first, it is barely able to break the surface because of its buoyant, fluffy fur. Determinedly, the pup tries again and again to fight this corklike bobbing until practice makes perfect. When it finally reaches bottom, the first sign of feeding behavior shows in the bits of kelp, pebbles, or starfish it proudly brings to the surface. In this manner, the pup securely spends its first year. When it is almost two-thirds its mother's size, it is finally able to paddle forth on its own.

Few animals prey on the sea otter. Sharks and killer whales have been known to kill them, and bald eagles are said to carry off the young. However, death by starvation is a more subtle "predator." On Amchitka, where the sea otters have increased, food resources have dwindled. This food scarcity, when combined with the violent winter storms of the Pacific, causes a period of great stress for the sea otters each year. High mortality occurs from late winter to early spring, particularly among large juvenile otters which are newly separated from their mothers and find themselves unable to survive the extreme conditions alone.

In captivity, the sea otter seems to survive well enough, although so far without breeding success. One early transplant survived in a freshwater pool at Seattle's Woodland Park Zoo for six years until an infestation of nasal mites (never found in the wild) overcame her. This suggested that salt water would provide a better captive environment. Today there are two sea otters at the Vancouver Aquarium, three at Tacoma's Aquarium, and three at San Diego's Sea World — all in salt water. All have shown an interest or made attempts at breeding, with the Tacoma otters coming closest to success. At Tacoma, there has been at least one full-term pup born. Unfortunately, it was drowned several days later, presumably because of some unknown interaction between the adult otters.

Today, man's pollutants — in the form of oil and industrial wastes — will no doubt have their deadly effect on this animal. But the staunch and sturdy sea otter has survived stormy seas and rough waters before. Now it appears that, with careful tending and management, the weasel family's fair-haired child will be with us for a long time.

Bibliography

BAILEY, JANE H., *The Sea Otter's Struggle* (Chicago, Follett Publishing Company, 1973), 95 pp. The sea otter's survival seen from aspects of evolution and the fur stampede.

BRANDER, R. B. and D. J. BOOKS, "Return of the Fisher," *Natural History,* vol. LXXXII (1973), no. 1, pp. 52-58.

BURNS, JOHN J., "Comparisons of Two Populations of Mink from Alaska," *Canadian Journal of Zoology,* vol. 42 (1964), pp. 1071-1079.

CAHALANE, VICTOR H., *Mammals of North America* (New York, Macmillan Company, 1968), 682 pp. Illustrated, authorative guide to principal species of mammals of North America. Written for the layman by a distinguished mammalogist.

EWER, R. F., *The Carnivores* (Ithaca, Cornell University Press, 1973), 494 pp. Anatomy from a functional aspect of the world's carnivores. For those interested in carnivore biology, ecology, and behavior.

FORTENBERY, DONALD K., "Characteristics of the Black-Footed Ferret," *U.S. Department of the Interior, Fish and Wildlife Resource Publication No. 109* (1972), 8 pp.

HALL, E. RAYMOND, "The Graceful and Rapacious Weasel," *Natural History,* vol. LXXX (1974), no. 9, pp. 44-50.

HALL, E. RAYMOND and KEITH R. KELSON, *Mammals of North America,* vol. II, "The Mustelidae" (New York, The Ronald Press, 1959), 1083 pp.

HARRIS, C. J., *A Study of the Recent Lutrinae* (London, Weidenfeld and Nicolson, 1968), 397 pp. Natural history of all the world's otters — taxonomy, physiology, behavior, etc.

HENDERSON, F. ROBERT, PAUL F. SPRINGER, and RICHARD ADRIAN, "The Black-Footed Ferret in South Dakota," *South Dakota Department of Game, Fish, and Parks Technical Bulletin No. 4* (1974), 37 pp.

INGLES, LLOYD G., *Mammals of the Pacific States* (Stanford, Stanford University Press, 1965), 506 pp.

IRVINE, GEORGE W., LESTER T. MAGNUS, and BERNARD J. BRADLE, "The Restocking of Fisher in Lake States Forests," *Transactions of the 29th North American Wildlife Conference* (1964), pp. 307-315.

KENYON, KARL, "The Sea Otter in the Eastern Pacific Ocean," U.S. Fish and Wildlife Service, *North American Fauna* No. 68 (1969), 352 pp.

LIERS, EMIL, "My Friends the Land Otters," *Natural History,* vol. LX (1951), no. 7, p. 320.

LIERS, EMIL, "Notes on the River Otter," *Journal of Mammalogy,* vol. 32 (1951), no. 1, pp. 1-9.

LINDER, RAYMOND L., ROBERT B. DAHLGREN, and CONRAD N. HILLMAN, "Black-Footed Ferret-Prairie Dog Inter-relationships," *Symposium on Rare and Endangered Wildlife of the Southwest U.S.* (Santa Fe, New Mexico Department of Game and Fish, 1972), 36 pp.

McCRACKEN, HAROLD, *Hunters of the Stormy Sea* (London, Oldbourne Press, 1957), 312 pp. The saga of the sea otter hunters and the 100-year rule of the Russians in the Pacific Northwest.

McNULTY, FAITH, *Must They Die?* (New York, National Audubon Society and Ballantine Books, 1972), 124 pp. The plight of the black-footed ferret as a casualty in the federal government's poisoning campaign against the prairie dog.

MADSON, JOHN, "Dark Days in Dogtown," *Audubon,* vol. 70 (1968), pp. 32-43.

MATTHIESSEN, PETER, *Wildlife in America* (New York, Viking Press, 1969), 304 pp. A popular history of North American fauna, with emphasis on the white man's effect on wildlife.

MAXHAM, GLENN, "Our Legendary Wolverine—Fiction or Fact?" *Minnesota Volunteer* (1971), September-October, pp. 40-43.

NOWAK, RONALD M., "Return of the Wolverine," *National Parks and Conservation Magazine,* vol. 47 (1973), no. 2, pp. 20-23.

OLSON, HERMAN F., "Return of a Native," *Wisconsin Conservation Bulletin,* vol. 31 (1966), no. 3, pp. 22-23. Fisher transplants in Wisconsin and Michigan.

PARK, ED, *The World of the Otter* (Philadelphia, Lippincott Company, 1971), 159 pp. A generously illustrated book about the North American otter's lifestyle.

PERRY, MARY L., "Notes on a Captive Badger," *The Murrelet,* vol. 20 (1939), no. 3, p. 52.

QUICK, HORACE, "Notes on the Ecology of Weasels in Gunnison, Colorado," *Journal of Mammalogy,* vol. 32 (1951), no. 3, pp. 281-290.

RAUSCH, R.A. and A.M. PEARSON, "Notes on the Wolverine in Alaska and the Yukon Territory," *Journal of Wildlife Management,* vol. 36 (1972), no. 2, pp. 249-268.

SANDEGREN, FINN E., ELLEN W. CHU, and JUDSON E. VANDEVERE, "Maternal Behavior in the California Sea Otter," *Journal of Mammalogy,* vol. 54 (1973), no. 3, pp. 668-679.

VERTS, B. J., *Biology of the Striped Skunk* (Urbana, The University of Illinois Press, 1967), 218 pp. Detailed description of this species—food habits, reproduction, behavior, and movements.

YOCOM, CHARLES F., "Status of Marten in Northern California, Oregon, and Washington," *California Fish and Game,* vol. 60 (1974), no. 1, pp. 54-57.

YOCOM, CHARLES F., "Wolverine Records in the Pacific Coastal States and New Records for Northern California," *California Fish and Game,* vol. 59 (1973), no. 3, pp. 207-209.

YOCOM, CHARLES F. and MICHAEL T. McCOLLUM, "Status of the Fisher in Northern California, Oregon, and Washington," *California Fish and Game,* vol. 54 (1973), no. 4, pp. 305-309.

Other Pacific Search Books in Paperback

Why Wild Edibles? by Russ Mohney
How to find and identify nearly 100 easy-to-collect plants west of the Rockies, and how to prepare and enjoy them. Recipes range from arrowhead tubers saute to wood sorrel sauerkraut. Photos, many in color, and drawings aid in identification. 320 pages, $6.95.

The Carrot Cookbook by Ann Saling
What can I do with the lowly carrot? This cookbook transforms a ho-hum, humdrum vegetable into a gourmet's delight with over 200 mouth-watering recipes. Historically, carrots have long been considered an aphrodisiac, so don't say we didn't warn you! 160 pages, $3.50.

The Green Tomato Cookbook by Paula Simmons
When you think "green tomato," if the only recipes that come to mind are "relish" and "fried tomatoes," try these more than 80 imaginative recipes for that bumper crop of green tomatoes. Pick tomatoes green on purpose. 96 pages, $2.95.

The Zucchini Cookbook by Paula Simmons
For year 'round good eating — think zucchini! This revised and enlarged second edition of a bestseller contains over 150 tasty recipes for that prolific vegetable— from zucchini chocolate cake to zucchini tetrazzini. 160 pages, $3.50.

Wild Mushroom Recipes by the Puget Sound Mycological Society
For you who enjoy the pleasure of the search, the serendipity of discovery, the gourmet dreams of the succulent fruits of the earth. More than 200 imaginative recipes give the cultivated variety a special elegance as well. 178 pages, $6.95.

Minnie Rose Lovgreen's Recipe for Raising Chickens by Minnie Rose Lovgreen
"The main thing is to keep them happy" is Minnie Rose's secret. She offers sixty years of her own experience to help you get started, telling how a hen talks with her chicks, even while they're still in the shell, and why chickens take dust baths (to keep down fleas). 32 pages, $2.00.

QL
737
C25
H16

Haley, Delphine.
   Sleek & savage : North America's weasel family / by Delphine Haley ; ⟨drawings by Maxine Morse⟩. — Seattle : Pacific Search Books, 1975.
   128 p. : ill. (some col.) ; 21 cm.

   Bibliography: p. 125-127.
   ISBN 0-914718-12-6 : $5.50

1. Mustelidae.   2. Mammals—North America.   I. Title.

QL737.C25H33   599'.74447'097   75-32837
                                                        MARC